The New Deal

Pulling America Out of the Great Depression

Titles in *The American Saga* series

Abolition of Slavery
Fighting for a Free America
0-7660-2605-1

America as a World Power
From the Spanish-American War to Today
0-7660-2606-X

Colonial America
Building Toward Independence
0-7660-2569-1

The History of U.S. Immigration
Coming to America
0-7660-2574-8

The Industrial Revolution
Manufacturing a Better America
0-7660-2571-3

The New Deal
Pulling America Out of the Great Depression
0-7660-2570-5

The Struggle for Equality
Women and Minorities in America
0-7660-2573-X

The Transcontinental Railroad and Westward Expansion
Chasing the American Frontier
0-7660-2572-1

★ *The American Saga*

The New Deal

Pulling America Out of the Great Depression

R. Conrad Stein

Enslow Publishers, Inc.
40 Industrial Road
Box 398
Berkeley Heights, NJ 07922
USA

http://www.enslow.com

Library of Congress Cataloging-in-Publication Data:

Stein, R. Conrad.
   The New Deal : pulling America out of the Great Depression /
R. Conrad Stein.
     p. cm. — (The American saga)
   Includes bibliographical references and index.
   ISBN 0-7660-2570-5
    1. New Deal, 1933–1939—Juvenile literature. 2. Depressions—1929—
United States—Juvenile literature. 3. United States—History—1919–1933—
Juvenile literature. 4. United States—History—1933–1945—Juvenile
literature. I. Title. II. Series.
E806.S784 2006
973.917—dc22

                                   2005022288

Printed in the United States of America

10 9 8 7 6 5 4 3 2 1

To Our Readers:
We have done our best to make sure all Internet Addresses in this book were
active and appropriate when we went to press. However, the author and the
publisher have no control over and assume no liability for the material available
on those Internet sites or on other Web sites they may link to. Any comments or
suggestions can be sent by e-mail to comments@enslow.com or to the address on
the back cover.

Illustration Credits: ©Adam Tanner/The Image Works, p. 111; ©Ann
Ronan Picture Library/HIP/The Image Works, p. 42; ©David H.
Wells/The Image Works, p. 56; Franklin Delano Roosevelt Library, pp. 41,
65, 113 (top); Harry S Truman Library, p. 48; Getty Images, pp. 49, 77,
81, 82, 92, 94, 114 (top); Hemera Technologies, Inc., p. 16; ©Larry
Mulvehill/The Image Works, p. 62; The Library of Congress, pp. 3, 9, 11,
18, 22, 27, 28, 30, 32, 36, 54, 60, 66, 70, 95, 97, 100, 106, 107, 113
(bottom), 114 (bottom); The National Archives and Records
Administration, pp. 6, 14.

Cover Illustration: The Library of Congress

Contents

This family from Amarillo, Texas, lived in a trailer without water or sanitation during the Great Depression.

Fear Itself

Once I built a railroad, I made it run.
Made it race against time.
Once I built a railroad, now it's done.
Brother, can you spare a dime?[1]

These lyrics are from the song "Brother, Can You Spare a Dime?" written in 1932 by E.Y. "Yip" Harburg. The song expressed the feelings of a once-proud working man who suddenly found himself unemployed, bewildered, and reduced to begging in the street.

Washington, D.C., was cloudy with a trace of sleet in the air on March 4, 1933. The grim weather matched the country's mood. At the time, one in four American workers was unemployed. Those who held jobs took pay cuts and lived in constant fear of being fired. Income for the country as a whole was less than half what it was in 1929. Children went to school hungry. Entire families were homeless. Men and women slept huddled in doorways and in empty railroad cars.

Inauguration Day

Despite this gloominess, crowds lined the streets to watch the presidential inaugural parade in 1933. At least the parade provided free entertainment for people without a dollar in their pockets. The skies began to clear when an open-topped limousine drove slowly down Pennsylvania Avenue. Sitting in the car were President Herbert Hoover and President-elect Franklin Roosevelt. In front and behind the limousine, marching bands played patriotic music. This was Inauguration Day, when an outgoing president officially passes power to a new commander-in-chief. Normally, Inauguration Day was viewed as a time of rebirth, a chance for fresh hope. But the people did little cheering. Grinding poverty and fear weakened the American spirit.

In fact, a feeling of tension hung in the air over Washington. The general public feared that law and order would break down and angry men and women would rise up in revolution. Just three weeks earlier in Miami, Florida, an unemployed bricklayer tried to shoot Roosevelt. The gunman missed and instead killed Chicago mayor Anton Cermak who sat beside the president-elect. The assassin acted alone and represented no political group. But all over the country radical organizations urged poor people to forcefully take over the government. The Communist Party was still a tiny force in America. Communists called for government ownership of factories and farms. Unemployed workers, who years earlier rejected Communism, began to listen to the party's message.

Early 1933 was one of the worst periods of the massive economic slump called the Great Depression. The

President-elect Franklin D. Roosevelt (right) and outgoing president Herbert Hoover rode in the same car during the inaugural parade. This is a tradition that is still observed today.

slump began in 1929 when the stock market collapsed. The stock market's sudden downturn wiped out profits for millions of investors and set off a chain of ruinous events. Banks closed and families were unable to withdraw the savings they had worked a lifetime to build. Factories shut down. Homeowners lost their homes because they could not pay their mortgages. Renters were thrown out on the streets along with all their furniture. Farms that had been owned by the same family for generations were sold to strangers because the farmers simply could not meet their bills.

By midmorning, the new president reached the inaugural stand. Roosevelt was helped forward while clutching the arm of his son James. Years earlier, Franklin Roosevelt had lost the use of his legs due to polio. Some Americans of the time questioned whether a man who was unable to walk could properly lead the nation in a time of such peril. Despite the cold on Inauguration Day, Roosevelt stood on the platform without a coat or hat. An estimated one hundred thousand people watched. Millions more listened on radio.

Speaking in rich tones, Roosevelt urged the people to have confidence in their country: "This great nation will endure as it has endured, will revive and will prosper."[2] He then said words which made the 1933 inaugural address stand out as one of the greatest American speeches ever made: "So, first of all, let me assert my firm belief that the only thing we have to fear is fear itself—nameless, unreasoning, unjustified terror which paralyzes needed efforts to convert retreat into advance."[3]

The crowd grew silent as people listened. Too many other politicians had tried to write off the current problem as a temporary reversal of fortunes. This new president said, "The people of the United States have not failed. . . . They have asked for discipline and direction under leadership. They have made me the present instrument of their wishes. In the spirit of the gift I take it."[4]

Applause and cheers greeted the conclusion of the speech. Still, people around the nation doubted the

Roosevelt (behind podium) is sworn in as president by Charles E. Hughes, chief justice of the Supreme Court.

Roosevelt administration could make a significant difference in their lives. The scars of the Great Depression ran too deep. Americans lacked hope the economy would ever improve. Also, a feeling of distrust in government prevailed. The government often took a long time to put programs into action.

This time, however, the skeptics were wrong. The day after Roosevelt took office he launched a revolutionary program called the New Deal. Suddenly, Washington sprang to life with dozens of new agencies and projects designed to get the economy moving again. Experienced observers of government were astonished by the speed with which the New Deal spirit gripped the capital. A flurry of laws were passed in Roosevelt's first one hundred days in office. To this day, historians debate whether the New Deal actually lifted the country out of the Great Depression. However, all agree that the New Deal of the 1930s was one of the most ambitious efforts ever made by the United States government to save the country from economic disaster.

The 1920s: The Boom That Busted

Night or daytime,
It's all playtime,
Ain't we got fun?
Hot or cold days,
Any old days,
Ain't we got fun?[1]

These lyrics from the song "Ain't We Got Fun?" were written in 1921. The song remained popular throughout the 1920s. "Ain't We Got Fun?" reflected the party-loving, carefree spirit of the decade.

The Roaring Twenties

In 1919, Americans celebrated victory in World War I. Returning soldiers paraded down city streets while bands played "When Johnny Comes Marching Home." American involvement in the conflict began in April 1917. The war ended when Germany signed an armistice on November 11, 1918. More than 116,000 Americans

This illustration on the February 18, 1926 *Life* magazine cover shows a flapper and an older man doing the Charleston. The Charleston was a popular dance in the 1920s.

were killed during nineteen months of warfare. When the rigors of the war were over, politicians, especially those of the Republican Party, promised the nation a "return to normalcy." However, the 1920s proved to be anything but a normal decade.

The ten-year span was called the Roaring Twenties. It was a time of fads, folly, zany antics, and ballyhoo. A new music called jazz was brought from the South by African-American musicians and became popular throughout the nation. Young people spoke their own language: "You're the cat's meow," described a particularly charming person; "You're a flat tire"[2] meant someone who is dull and boring.

This time of fun and frolic was fueled by a booming economy. New products appeared and a growing middle class eagerly bought them. Before the 1920s, the automobile was thought of as a plaything for the rich. Then, in 1924, Henry Ford dropped the price of his Model T car to $290. At the reduced price, even a worker in Ford's factory could afford a Model T. Other carmakers also produced cheaper autos. By 1929, 23 million cars jammed the nation's roads, triple the number at the start of the decade.

Electricity also entered American homes. In 1920, only one-third of the nation's households enjoyed electricity. By 1929, two-thirds of American homes had access to electricity. Families bought electric vacuum cleaners, washing machines, and other labor-saving devices. Demand for the new machines produced thousands of factory jobs. Prosperity fed on prosperity.

At first, Model T Fords were only available in black.

Radio joined the list of miraculous new products. As late as 1919, radio was a hobby tinkered with by a few people in their basement workshops. The hobbyists wore earphones and fussed over crystal sets while trying to tune in to some far-off signal. Early in the 1920s loudspeakers were developed and radio moved into the living room. Sales of radio sets soared from $2 million in 1920 to $600 million in 1929. The radio explosion generated jobs. Radio also changed American entertainment habits. Main streets were strangely empty in the evening when families stayed home to listen to popular shows such as *True Detective Mysteries*. By the end of the decade, 618 radio stations were in operation.[3]

In the 1920s, most young men and young women

lived better than their parents had ever dreamed of living. Yet many sectors of the population suffered poverty despite the general good times. Low-paid factory workers could not afford to buy the products they manufactured. Economists would later cite the sharp division between rich and poor as one of the root causes of the Great Depression.

Farmers, African Americans, and immigrants were among those who were denied their share of wealth in the Roaring Twenties. During World War I, the nation's farmers thrived. Wartime demand for food drove crop prices upward. After the war, crop prices dropped sharply. Farmers could not pay their bills. Many frustrated farmers moved to cities to take factory jobs. In the mid-1920s, the city population grew larger than the farm population for the first time in United States history.

The vast majority of the nation's 10.5 million African Americans lived in the South during the 1920s. There they were forced to take low-paying jobs and suffer other kinds of discrimination because of the color of their skin. African Americans began what came to be called the "great migration" to the northern states, only to discover they still faced job and housing discrimination.

In the early 1900s, immigrants flooded to the United States at the rate of almost one million a year. Most of the newcomers were from southern or eastern Europe. The immigrants had little education and few job skills. They settled in the cities, toiled in factories, and lived in whatever housing they could afford. By the

Most immigrants came to America by boat. These people traveled from eastern Europe on the U.S.S. *Amsterdam*.

1920s, every large city had sprawling immigrant slums. In those slums throngs of people lived in poverty.

The Roaring Twenties was a decade of haves and have-nots. Yet even poor Americans believed the overall prosperity of the times would someday lift their fortunes too. Through most of the 1920s, wages and national income rose. Times were good. Hopes were high.

The Stock Market, A Fountain of Riches

Investors have bought and sold stocks for hundreds of years. The first European stock market was established in Antwerp, Belgium, in 1531. The New York

Stock Exchange was established in 1792. At a stock exchange, individual investors buy shares of a company in the form of certificates called stock. This way, a person who buys stock in a company becomes a partial owner of that company. In theory, if the company does well the price of its stock will rise. The person who owns shares of the stock may sell them at anytime. By selling at the right time the investor can make a tidy sum of money. Of course, if the company does poorly, its stock price will fall. Then, the investor who sells the stock loses money if he or she had bought it for a higher price.

The strength of the demand for stocks governs share prices on a stock exchange. A company need not be turning profits to see its shares rise in price. Many investors will buy shares in a young and struggling firm and gamble that it will have a great future. This tactic allows a person to buy into a company when its share price is low. An investor can do well by buying stock at a low price and selling the shares as the price rises. But the element of chance is always present. No one can accurately tell when or if a company's share price will go up or down, just as no one can predict whether a certain horse will win a race.

In the late 1920s, the stock market looked like a race where many horses were destined to win. From 1925 to 1929, the average price of shares sold on the New York Stock Exchange doubled. Prices of individual stocks skyrocketed. A single share of General Electric, which cost $150 in 1920, shot up to $1,600 in late summer 1929. In 1929 alone, shares in National Cash Register Company rose from \$59 to \$114. That same year, the price of Sears, Robuck shares climbed from \$80 to \$181, and U.S. Steel shares rose from \$150 to \$261.[4]

The stock market became one of the most exciting subjects of conversation in American life. Only a small percentage of the population actively engaged in buying and selling stocks. No matter. People followed the rising stock market with the same zeal that they watched their favorite baseball team.

Danger lurked in this money mill. Banks loaned money to investment firms which in turn put the money into the stock market. Individual investors engaged in a practice called buying on margin. A person buying stocks on margin provided only a small down payment of the purchase price. Often, an investor could buy stock by putting up just 10 percent of the stock's value. This system created paper fortunes for some investors. If stock prices dropped, however, the margin-buyer would be left with a crushing debt.

Faith in the future prevailed during this decade. Most Americans held steady jobs. Even low-paid factory hands dreamed about someday buying an automobile or a home. In August 1928, Herbert Hoover accepted the Republican nomination for president and told the party convention, "We in America today are nearer to the final triumph over poverty than ever before in the history of any land."[5] Few argued with Hoover's optimistic declaration.

Crash!

In September 1929, prices on the stock market dipped sharply. Many investors had chosen September to sell their shares and reap the profits. In a matter of days, the market recovered once again. Veterans of New York's Wall Street, where many banks and financial institutions stood, accepted these ups and downs as the normal course of business. Share prices were expected to fluctuate. Then, a wave of selling in early October left investors shaken. Some observers predicted a large-scale decline in stock prices. Few people imagined the disaster to come.

On Thursday, October 24, 1929, the landslide started. The morning session on stock exchanges saw higher than normal selling volume. Panic set in as stock prices plummeted. Hysterical investors desperately fought each other to get to telephones. They wanted to call in orders selling their shares before the market plunged even farther. That day was forever

"How could I lose $100,000? I never had $100,000."

—A victim of the 1929 stock market crash.

called Black Thursday on Wall Street. It was followed by Terrifying Tuesday, October 29. On that one day, more than 16 million shares were traded and the *New York Times* estimated eight billion dollars in paper value vanished.[6]

By mid-November 1929, stock prices had fallen

STAGE BROADWAY SCREEN

VARIETY

PRICE 25¢·

Published Weekly at 154 West 46th St., New York, N. Y., by Variety, Inc. Annual subscription, $10. Single copies, 25 cents.
Entered as second-class matter December 22, 1905, at the Post Office at New York, N. Y., under the act of March 3, 1879.

VOL. XCVII. No. 3   NEW YORK, WEDNESDAY, OCTOBER 30, 1929   88 PAGES

WALL ST. LAYS AN EGG

Going Dumb Is Deadly to Hostess In Her Serious Dance Hall Profesh | DROP IN STOCKS ROPES SHOWMEN | Kidding Kissers in Talkers Burns Up Fans of Screen's Best Lover

This headline on the cover of *Variety* was published on Wednesday, October 30, 1929, the day after the stock market crashed on "Terrifying Tuesday."

some 40 percent. Even the country's largest and most prestigious firms took heavy losses. General Electric lost $48 per share and Westinghouse dropped $34. Investors, large and small, were stunned by the sudden crash. Particularly hard-hit were the amateur investors who had bought stocks on margin and were now deeply in debt. Many small investors, who did not understand the system very well to begin with, were bewildered by the development. One woman, who had bought on margin, told her stockbroker, "How could I lose $100,000? I never had $100,000."[7]

The crash in the fall of 1929 was the worst in the long history of stock exchange operations. Economists still argue about exactly what happened in that fateful October. For years, some experts warned that stocks were overvalued. Yet, as long as prices went up, they hung onto

Stock Losses

Here is a list of how share prices of ten major companies fared between their high point of September 3, 1929, before the crash, and November 13, 1929, two weeks after the crash. The prices have been rounded to the nearest dollar:

	September 3, 1929	November 13, 1929
American Can	$182	$86
American Telephone & Telegraph	$304	$197
Anaconda Copper	$132	$70
Electric Bond & Share	$187	$50
General Motors	$73	$36
Montgomery Ward	$138	$49
New York Central	$256	$160
Union Carbide & Carbon	$138	$59
U.S. Steel	$262	$150
Woolworth	$100	$52[8]

their shares to take advantage of the rising tide. Then, prices tumbled and fear took over. In a frenzy, thousands sold their stocks while they could at least get some value out of them. A cloud of gloom settled over Wall Street. Investors who salvaged a few dollars in the crash refused to put money back into the failing economy.

At first, the stock market collapse had little direct effect on the lives of average Americans. Factory workers reported to their jobs. Farmers toiled in the fields as always. Then, New Years Eve, 1929, came, ending the Roaring Twenties. The parties were more subdued. The great energy of the roaring years was somehow missing. Americans sensed the good times were over. The economy was now on an uncertain and perhaps an ominous course.

Hard Times

> *We thought American business was the Rock of Gibraltar. We were the prosperous nation and nothing could stop us now ... Suddenly the big dream exploded. The impact was unbelievable.*[1]
>
> E.Y. "Yip" Harburg, the songwriter who wrote "Brother, Can You Spare a Dime?"

The Great Depression

Economic reversals, called depressions, occur regularly in America and in other countries with a free enterprise system. A depression begins when people and businesses cut back on their spending. Spending patterns often change due to investment failures such as the crash of 1929. Even the Roaring Twenties had its own earlier depression when crop prices collapsed in 1920 and 1921 and ruined the lives of many farm families.

In 1930, the sudden extreme lapse in spending

brought about by the stock market crash slowed down American business. This began a nationwide spending freeze which had a terrible snowballing effect. For example, after seeing others lose their jobs, a family might decide not to buy a new radio. This meant someone at the radio factory was fired, when the demand for radios declined. Jobless factory workers could not spend money at the grocery store. This meant less work for grocery store employees.

Uncertainty in the future bred a fear which ultimately paralyzed the economy. Americans were simply afraid of spending money. By 1933, the Hollywood thriller *King Kong* played to empty theaters. Few people would part with the ten cents it cost to buy a movie ticket.

Previous depressions ended after a year or so and the economy rebounded. This time the economic picture grew worse each month. In the dismal winter of 1932–1933, jobless men and women were seen wandering the streets in their ragged coats. Many had newspapers stuffed in their shoes to cover up holes. The hordes of poor made no sense in America, the richest country on Earth. Newspaper writers began calling this economic catastrophe the Great Depression.

Never before had the nation experienced unemployment of this magnitude. In 1925, only 3 percent of American workers were jobless. By 1930, that figure had climbed to almost 9 percent. Two years later, 25 percent were without jobs. Those who clung to

With outstretched hands, these men ask for jobs outside an International Longshoreman's & Warehousemen's Union building in the early 1930s.

jobs were forced to take pay cuts. The Briggs Manufacturing Company in Detroit paid male factory hands 10 cents an hour and women 4 cents an hour.[2] Yet Briggs and similar companies had long lines of people asking—sometimes begging—to be hired.

Out-of-work Americans turned to side occupations to bring in some money. Many sold apples on street corners. Women washed clothes for as little as a dime a day. Children returned pop bottles (when they could find an empty one in an alley) to get a two-cent deposit. Hundreds of men and teenagers in New York

The Apple Sellers

People selling apples from sidewalk stands became sad symbols of the Great Depression. The practice began in 1930, when apple growers enjoyed an abundant crop, but could not sell them to a public worried about spending. An organization called the International Apple Shipper's Association agreed to give apples on credit to the unemployed in hopes they could sell them. At the stands, the apples sold for about a nickel apiece. Supposedly some of the apple sellers included ruined bankers, stockbrokers, and heads of companies.[3]

People selling apples in Jacksonville, Texas

City took to shining shoes for a living. The price for a shoeshine in New York dropped to five cents.

Chaos ruled the banking business. During the good times, bankers used customers' savings to invest in the stock market. Then came the crash of 1929, and over the next three years the value of stocks fell 80 percent. In 1930, some 1,350 banks closed and could not repay the people who had deposited money in savings accounts. New York City's Bank of the United States shut its doors in December 1930. This marked the largest bank failure in U.S. history up to that time. The Bank of the United States held the savings of many working-class immigrants. When it failed, some four hundred thousand people lost their savings.[4] More than two thousand additional banks failed in 1931. Across the nation nervous savers started what was called a "run on the banks." People rushed into the banks that were still open demanding their savings in cash. These withdrawals worsened the problem of bank failure. Many Americans lost funds they had been accumulating all their lives.

Sudden poverty changed the face of America. In big cities, men and women stood in long "breadlines" to purchase day-old bread at a reduced price from a baker. Tenants who failed to pay their rent were routinely thrown out of their apartments by landlords. Evicted families sitting on the sidewalk surrounded by their furniture became a common sight. The vacant look in the eyes of the suddenly homeless served as a pitiful reminder of the economic tragedy.

A long breadline stretches down the street from the McCauley Water Street Mission in Brooklyn, New York. The mission was founded by a reformed ex-convict and still provides food for the needy today.

In its full force, the Great Depression struck with the impact of a natural disaster such as a flood or a hurricane. Prosperous, hardworking Americans were stunned to find themselves jobless and their savings wiped out by bank failures. Families pawned wedding rings and sold prized furniture in a desperate attempt to keep roofs over their heads. A woman from Cleveland, who once had lived in a large house, wrote, "My father lost his job and we moved into a double-garage. . . . It was awful cold when you opened those garage doors. We would sleep with rugs and blankets over the top of us."[5]

For the first time in memory, masses of Americans faced hunger. The writer Edmund Wilson visited a working-class Chicago neighborhood and reported,

> There is not a garbage dump in Chicago which is not diligently haunted by the hungry. Last summer in the hot weather when the smell was sickening and the flies were thick, there were a hundred people a day coming to one of the dumps, falling on the heap of refuse as soon as the truck had pulled out and digging in it with sticks and hands.[6]

In West Virginia a schoolteacher noticed a sickly-looking girl in her class and told her to go home and get something to eat. The girl replied, "I can't. It's my sister's turn to eat."[7]

President Hoover Reacts

In every election during the 1920s, Americans chose Republican presidents. Most of those presidents enjoyed a solidly Republican Congress. The Republicans ruled according to their philosophy of government: Let the open market determine prices, wages, and the level of employment. Party regulars believed that American business, if given a free hand, would provide for the people's well-being. This practice seemed to have worked in the 1920s, the most prosperous decade in American history. Then the Great Depression upset American business operations like nothing else had before. Businesses closed by the hundreds. In 1932, the nation's steelmaking plants were operating at only one-eighth of their capacity.

High-rise construction projects, started in the 1920s, now stood idle. Naked steel skeletons of incomplete buildings rose on city streets. The skeletons stood, lonely-looking, while their steel framing became coated with rust.

The Republican Herbert Clark Hoover (1874–1964) served as president in the darkest days of the Great Depression. Born in Iowa, Hoover was the son of a Quaker blacksmith. He worked as a farmhand and an office boy while saving money to study engineering. As a young man, he traveled the world and became a millionaire operating mines. Then, public service called to Hoover. During World War I, he led the U.S. Food Administration. His genius for organization helped to feed thousands of starving Europeans.

President Herbert Hoover

Hoover was by all measures an intelligent and a caring man. Yet, a great many Americans blamed the president for not curing the nation's ills during the worst times of the Great Depression. The tar-paper shacks where homeless people lived were called "Hoovervilles." Newspapers with which the unemployed covered themselves at night became "Hoover blankets." The paper sacks that held the spare clothing of jobless people as they looked for work were "Hoover bags."

The stock market crash and the Great Depression began less than a year into Hoover's presidency. He hoped to fix the problem through traditional Republican measures: leave businesses alone and let American enterprise restore the economy. Hoover urged American companies not to cut the wages of their employees. However, he refused to back laws designed to protect a worker's paycheck. The policy of allowing the economy to fix itself failed miserably in the early 1930s.

The Hoover administration did approve some measures to help businesses and speed up the recovery process. In 1932, Congress founded the Reconstruction Finance Corporation (RFC). The RFC loaned money to banks and companies to keep them in operation. Critics claimed the RFC was a Republican attempt to fix things by starting from the top. The critics demanded: What about the people on the bottom?

Hoover opposed using federal government funds to give direct aid to the country's poor. American tradition said that private charities should help the unfortunate. Charitable organizations responded by setting up soup kitchens which gave out-of-work people a bowl of soup and a few slices of bread. In New York City, lines at one soup kitchen wove through Times Square. Alongside the hungry soup kitchen customers were lines of well-to-do men and women waiting to buy theater tickets. State and local governments gave money to poor people in the form of weekly allotments. Called relief payments, they were barely enough to keep a family alive.

The Hoover administration backed several large public works projects. The projects were designed to provide jobs as well as to improve the quality of life. Thousands of construction workers labored on the Boulder Dam (now called the Hoover Dam). This gigantic dam was built across the Colorado River. When completed in 1936, the dam controlled flooding and its generators provided electricity for states in the West. Most Americans approved of the Boulder Dam and other such projects. The Democratic Party and spokesmen for the unemployed called for more such public works to provide jobs.

Desperation in America

Depression conditions caused the American mood to turn dangerously ugly. Unemployed people staged hunger marches in several cities. A near-riot broke out in hard-hit Detroit as jobless autoworkers demonstrated in front of the Ford plant. In 1931, hundreds of men and women in Minneapolis stormed a grocery store and looted food from its shelves. Another hungry mob raided a grocery store in Oklahoma city. Yet most Americans remained law-abiding. People walked about with little worry for their personal safety in city slums

"Beans, Bacon, and Gravy"

Hunger is rarely a joke, but Americans suffering through the Great Depression were eager to laugh at just about anything. A lively song called "Beans, Bacon, and Gravy" was sung in the early 1930s. No one knows who wrote the song. In an almost lighthearted manner it tells the plight of a middle-age man who could afford nothing but the most basic and monotonous food. The song was especially popular with the poor. Of course, many poor people lacked even the money to buy cheap beans and bacon:

I was born long ago
In eighteen ninety-one,
And I've seen many a panic, I will own.
I've been hungry, I've been cold,
And now I'm growing old,
But the worst I've seen is nineteen thirty-one.

Chorus
Oh, those beans, bacon, and gravy,
They almost drive me crazy!
I eat them till I see them in my dreams.
When I wake up in the morning
And another day is dawning,
Then I know I'll have another mess of beans.[8]

Members of the Bonus Army sit in Protest on the lawn of the Capitol Building.

as well as in suburbs. Street crime, even in the height of the depression, was not a problem.

In 1932, a group of men called the Bonus Army marched on Washington. The group was made up of about fifteen thousand World War I veterans. The men descended on the nation's capital demanding pension bonuses for their wartime service. Such bonuses were promised by the government, but they were not payable until 1945. The veterans, most of whom were unemployed, insisted their bonuses be issued at once. President Hoover opposed the idea of granting bonuses. He ordered police and troops to rid the capital of the protesting veterans. In a confrontation with Washington police on July 28, two protesters were shot and killed.[9] Soldiers burned down the shacks the veterans had set up near Washington. Commanding the soldiers was one of America's most famous army leaders, General Douglas MacArthur. He was assisted by a little-known major named Dwight D. Eisenhower, who would later become president. Eisenhower criticized his one-time boss for the heavy-handed tactics he used against the Bonus Army.

The Bonus Army was one of many embarrassments the Hoover administration suffered in the opening years of the Great Depression. Yet even Hoover's harshest critics found it difficult to personally blame the president for the tragic times. Aides claimed Hoover worked long hours trying to cure the nation's ills. He conferred with experts and read reports about conditions around the country. Still, the president stubbornly held to the policy that the free enterprise system would eventually right the ship and deliver the American people from the depths of poverty.

That Man, FDR

Franklin Delano Roosevelt, born in 1882, never experienced poverty in his life. He traced his family back to Klaes Martensen van Roosevelt, a Dutch merchant who bought land in New York City in the 1600s. Theodore Roosevelt, the twenty-sixth president of the United States, was Franklin's distant cousin. Franklin grew up in a mansion overlooking the Hudson River in New York State. He was attended by maids and schooled by private tutors. Often, he accompanied his parents on trips to Europe where he learned to speak German and French.

Roosevelt graduated from Harvard in 1903. He then attended law school there and became a lawyer in New York. In 1905, he married Eleanor Roosevelt, another distant cousin. From the start, young Roosevelt gravitated toward politics. He joined the Democratic Party as his father had, and in 1910 he ran for the New York State Senate in a district that had been controlled by Republicans for more than fifty years. The twenty-nine-year-old Roosevelt astonished the experts by winning the Senate seat. In office, he boldly fought the political bosses who ran New York City.

In 1913, President Woodrow Wilson appointed Roosevelt assistant secretary of the Navy. This was a delightful assignment because Roosevelt always had a love for ships and the sea. In his navy post, he earned the reputation as a man willing to take charge of tasks and make quick decisions. Roosevelt ran for vice president on the ticket with James Cox in 1920 and lost. But the 1920 presidential campaign thrust Roosevelt into the national spotlight. Tall and handsome, the voters took note of this wealthy young man from New York. Newspaper headlines began referring to Franklin D. Roosevelt affectionately by his initials—FDR.

The Scourge of Polio

Polio is often called infantile paralysis because it commonly strikes children between 4 and 15 years of age. Polio also can affect adults. It is caused by a virus that enters the body through the nose or mouth. The disease attacks the central nervous system. Some types of polio will kill or leave a victim permanently crippled.

Through much of the twentieth century Americans lived in fear of polio because it struck so quickly and attacked so many children. In the 1930s and 1940s, many Americans believed the disease could be caught in swimming pools. This mistaken belief about swimming pools spread largely because Franklin Roosevelt's polio struck shortly after he went swimming. In 1955, Dr. Jonas E. Salk of the University of Pittsburgh developed a vaccine that protected people from the disease. Polio, once a major scourge throughout the world, has been under control in the United States through the use of Salk vaccine.

In August 1921, Roosevelt visited his family's summer home in New Brunswick, Canada. He tumbled into the water while sailing and got chilled. The next day when he went swimming, he felt unusually tired. Suddenly his left leg refused to function. Then his right leg also lost feeling. Spasms of pain rushed up and down his back. Doctors were called. Eventually Franklin Roosevelt learned his diagnosis: He had the crippling disease polio. Over the next few months, the conditioned worsened. The thirty-nine-year-old Franklin D. Roosevelt completely lost the use of his legs.

After enduring a period of deep mental depression, Roosevelt devoted his energies to physical conditioning. Using gym equipment, he built up his arms. Roosevelt bragged he was now more muscular than Jack Dempsey, the reigning heavyweight boxer. His doctors fitted braces on his legs. With great effort he learned to walk at least a few steps on crutches. Swimming became his favorite sport. In 1926, he bought a swimming spa in Warm Springs, Georgia. He invited other people with polio to Warm Springs to swim with him. Many of those polio victims were impoverished and uneducated, but the wealthy Roosevelt swam and laughed with them. He especially enjoyed being with children who suffered from polio. He called the children "my gang."

In those days, political leaders liked to present an image of themselves as vigorous and energetic men. It seemed unlikely that Roosevelt, who could not walk, would seek high political office. But FDR was not afraid

Hidden Handicap

It was no secret that Roosevelt could not walk and that he moved mostly with the aid of a wheelchair. But FDR insisted he never be photographed in a wheelchair. When giving a speech he braced himself and stood upright even though standing was painful to him. Newspaper and newsreel photographers complied with his wishes. Few photographs exist of a wheelchair-bound Franklin Roosevelt.

This is one of the few pictures of Roosevelt in a wheelchair. He is talking to a family friend, Ruthie Bie, and holding his dog Fala.

President Franklin D. Roosevelt had a big task ahead of him: He had to pull America out of the Great Depression.

of breaking tradition. In 1924, he made a brilliant speech to nominate New York governor Al Smith as the Democratic candidate for president. Two years later, under the urging of Al Smith, he ran for governor of New York and won.

FDR served New York as governor when the Great Depression first gripped the country and his state. He battled with Republican legislators to channel more state funds into relief efforts for the state's poor. As the 1932 presidential election neared and the depression deepened, powerful Democrats suggested Roosevelt run for president.

In 1932, FDR won the presidential nomination of the Democratic Party. The Republicans renominated President Herbert Hoover. With millions of Americans unemployed and the Bonus Army in Washington, Hoover campaigned at a disadvantage. FDR waged a vigorous campaign. He visited thirty-eight states. In speech after speech he promised to address the needs of the "forgotten man" of the times. To him the forgotten men of the depression included the small business owner, the worker, and the farmer. Roosevelt won in a landslide. He carried forty-two of the forty-eight states (Alaska and Hawaii were not yet states).

During the 1932 campaign, FDR said little about the specific policies he would launch to end the Great Depression. He often attacked his opponent and the Republican Party. He criticized Hoover for doing too little to lift the country out of the depression. Then he said the president was spending too much money, and he sometimes made both points in the same speech. The people had no idea as to what they could expect from FDR. Therefore the New Deal, the most radical domestic program ever launched in America, came as a shock to many.

The New Deal Begins

I pledge you—I pledge myself to a new deal for the American people,[1]

Franklin Roosevelt declared in Chicago on July 2, 1932, when he accepted the Democratic Party's nomination for the office of president. He did not use the term "new deal" for several months after that speech. But the term endured. From the beginning, newspapers called Roosevelt's domestic programs the New Deal.

A Time of Peril

During the winter of 1932–1933, unemployment figures grew worse each week. In industrial centers such as Detroit, Michigan, more than 50 percent of the workforce was jobless. Breadlines were longer than ever before. Americans discussed revolution openly. Joe Morrison, a coal miner from Indiana, said, "People were talkin' revolution all over the place. You met guys ridin' the freight trains and so forth, talkin' about what they'd like to do with a machine gun. How they'd like to tear loose on the rich. . . ."[2]

The Roosevelt administration hoped to defuse this dangerous situation in two ways: first, by providing immediate cash for the needy, and second, by setting in motion long-term plans designed to get the economy moving again. In a rush of activity that began in March 1933, the New Deal created dozens of government agencies designed to accomplish these goals. The agencies were known by their abbreviations. Thus the government agencies were dubbed "alphabet soup" by newspaper writers. For example, the Home Owners Loan Corporation was called the HOLC. The HOLC gave loans to unemployed homeowners so they could meet their mortgage payments.

In mapping out the New Deal, the president was assisted by college professors, social workers, and respected economists. These experts were generally called Roosevelt's Brain Trust. Roosevelt remained the boss. Roosevelt demanded that the Brain Trust act with utmost speed. Sometimes the different New Deal agencies duplicated each other's work. No matter. The agencies still leaped into action. Before he became president, Roosevelt said, "The country needs . . . the country demands bold, persistent experimentation. It is common sense to take a method and try it: If it fails, admit it frankly and try another. But above all, try something."[3]

The First 100 Days

Fifteen major new laws were passed by Congress and signed by the president during Roosevelt's first three months in office. Journalists called this whirlwind period the First 100 Days. Washington politicians normally work at a slow pace. Because of the emergency, a blizzard of new measures were rushed through Congress in a very short span of time.

Upon taking office, the president faced a bank crisis. Since the crash of 1929, more than five thousand banks around the nation had closed. A fresh wave of bank failures in February 1933 led to increasing numbers of worried savers rushing to their banks to withdraw funds. To address the banking crisis, FDR called Congress into a special session on Sunday, March 5, 1933. This was the day after he was sworn in as president. Roosevelt announced a "bank holiday," and temporarily closed all banks. In the next few days the banks were allowed to reopen after government auditors examined their records and determined each institution was sound. This firm action ended the run on the banks. The banking system then resumed its normal operations.

Roosevelt's swift measures to shore up the banking system set the tone for the First 100 Days and the early New Deal. Roosevelt demanded immediate action to restore faith in banks, and Congress quickly complied. Roosevelt was fortunate in that his landslide victory in the 1932 elections produced a Democratic majority in Congress. Not all Democrats were New

Dealers, but not all Republicans opposed New Deal measures. Led by Roosevelt, Congress was charged with a new energy. It was as if the President had declared war on the depression. Waging the war became the patriotic duty of each member of Congress.

Roosevelt also appealed to the public to accept the New Deal. On March 12, he launched the first in a series of radio addresses called "fireside chats." Over the radio, Americans listened to their president as he explained the policies being created in Washington. The radio talks were informal. They were designed to make it appear the president was sitting inside a family living room, perhaps next to the fireplace. Radio was new, but Roosevelt seemed at home with the media. Eleanor Roosevelt once remarked, "His [FDR's] voice lent itself remarkably to the radio. It was a natural gift. . . ."[4] The President wrote most of

"... it is safer to keep your money in a reopened bank than under the mattress."

—President Roosevelt, in one of his fireside chats, assuring Americans that the banking system was safe.

the material he delivered in the fireside chats. He labored to keep his concepts easily understandable. When he declared the banking system sound, FDR told the radio audience, "it is safer to keep your money in a reopened bank than under the mattress."[5]

FDR delivered twenty-seven fireside chats during

This microphone was used by Roosevelt during his fireside chats. Around the microphone are transcripts of the speeches he gave during the chats.

the early 1930s. They were broadcast live from a studio in the basement of the White House. Through the radio, Roosevelt became a friendly and wise visitor in American homes. The radio "visits" brought broad, popular support for the New Deal.

One measure passed in the First 100 Days marked the end of Prohibition. In 1920, the 18th Amendment to the Constitution went into effect. It made illegal, or

During Prohibition, people who illegally made alcohol were called bootleggers. Here, in 1925, New York police arrest a group of men suspected of making illegal liquor. Roosevelt repealed Prohibition in 1933.

prohibited, the sale of alcoholic beverages in the United States. Prohibition laws were often violated. Illegal saloons and bars, called "speakeasies," sprang up in cities and towns. During his presidential campaign, Roosevelt promised to end Prohibition. In December 1933, Prohibition officially came to an end. Beer was sold, legally, for the first time in more than a decade. Roosevelt-backers pointed out that the renewed beer trade provided jobs. The government was also allowed to collect taxes from the now-legal saloons and bars.

Toward the end of March 1933, Congress created the Civilian Conservation Corps (CCC). The CCC sent unemployed young men into wilderness areas. The young men (ages seventeen to twenty-four) cut hiking trails, built fire watch stations, and planted trees.

In the First 100 Days, Congress established the Public Works Administration (PWA). The PWA was a huge agency which built schools, courthouses, and other public buildings. The building program was implemented as much to create jobs as to erect public structures.

Roosevelt and Congress took the country off the gold standard in April 1933. This broke a historic practice that had allowed people to freely exchange U.S. currency of twenty dollar bills or higher for gold at any national bank. Through Roosevelt's actions, paper money was now no longer backed by gold. Some economists feared this would make the currency useless. But paper money retained its buying power even after the country withdrew from the gold standard. Foreign trade became easier and the economy improved.

During the First 100 Days, the New Deal helped the nation's farmers by telling them, in effect, less is more. The Agricultural Adjustment Act (AAA) paid farmers not to grow crops or raise livestock in abundance. Farmers suffered because the oats, corn, and pigs they produced brought so little money on the open market. The AAA attempted to manipulate the market by limiting what the farmer could grow or raise. The public and the press protested. Critics claimed AAA policies would raise food prices and destroy the farmers' historic freedom to grow what they wished. Despite the complaints, the AAA stabilized farm prices. Reliable prices for crops allowed many small family farms to remain in operation.

"WE DO OUR PART."

—Text from the National Recovery Administration logo.

One of the most celebrated of the First 100 Day acts was the creation of the National Recovery Administration (NRA). A key element of the NRA was to encourage industry to retain workers instead of firing them. The NRA implored companies to pay their employees a living wage. Businesses which complied with NRA standards were given a proud symbol: a Blue Eagle with the words "WE DO OUR PART" underneath. The government asked Americans to buy products from businesses which displayed the Blue

Other Agencies and Acts Created as New Deal Legislation in the 1930s:

Agency	Founding	Description
Commodity Credit Corporation (CCC)	1933	Not to be confused with the Civilian Conservation Corps, this other CCC engaged in the buying and selling of farm products to keep crop prices stable.
Farm Credit Administration (FCA)	1933	The FCA gave long-term loans and short-term loans to farmers at affordable interest rates.
Farm Security Administration (FSA)	1937	The FSA granted loans to farmers so they could buy modern equipment.
Federal Communications Commission (FCC)	1934	This agency was established to regulate the radio, telephone, and telegraph industries; the FCC remains important today and also provides rules for television and radio broadcasters.
Federal Crop Insurance Corporation (FCIC)	1938	This agency allowed farmers to buy insurance against crop loss due to storms or blight.
Federal Housing Administration (FHA)	1934	One of two agencies which guaranteed homeowners loans to prevent eviction; in 1932 alone, some 250,000 American families lost their homes because they could not pay their mortgages.
National Youth Administration (NYA)	1935	This agency gave job-training and other classes to unemployed young people, ages sixteen to twenty-five.
Rural Electrification Administration (REA)	1935	In the 1930s, few American farmers enjoyed electricity in their houses because it was costly to build power lines into farm regions; the REA loaned money to power companies for the purpose of bringing electricity to rural areas.
United States Housing Authority (USHA)	1937	This agency was active in slum clearance (tearing down dilapidated buildings) and erecting low-cost housing units in the cities.

Eagle. Roosevelt launched the NRA with a burst of patriotic zeal. More than one thousand cities and towns held NRA parades. The greatest such parade was "Blue Eagle Day," held in New York City on September 13, 1933. Some 250,000 people marched while 1.5 million watched. A giant blimp, trailing a WE DO OUR PART banner, hovered over the New York parade route.[6]

The First 100 Days ended in June 1933. Congress continued to pass New Deal legislation in the months and years to come. In general, later New Deal acts dealt more with reforming the economy instead of providing immediate relief for the unemployed.

The impression of the First 100 Days remains an important legacy in American history. To this day, the record of a new president is reviewed after his first one hundred days in office. No president has matched the energy and pace Roosevelt achieved in his historic First 100 Days.

After The First 100 Days

The Securities and Exchange Commission (SEC) was established in 1934. The SEC attacked the major cause of the depression: the stock market crash. The SEC wrote laws governing the purchase of securities (stocks and bonds). Under SEC standards, corporations offering to sell shares had to make their financial records public. This allowed a potential buyer to determine what a company was worth. It was hoped that a

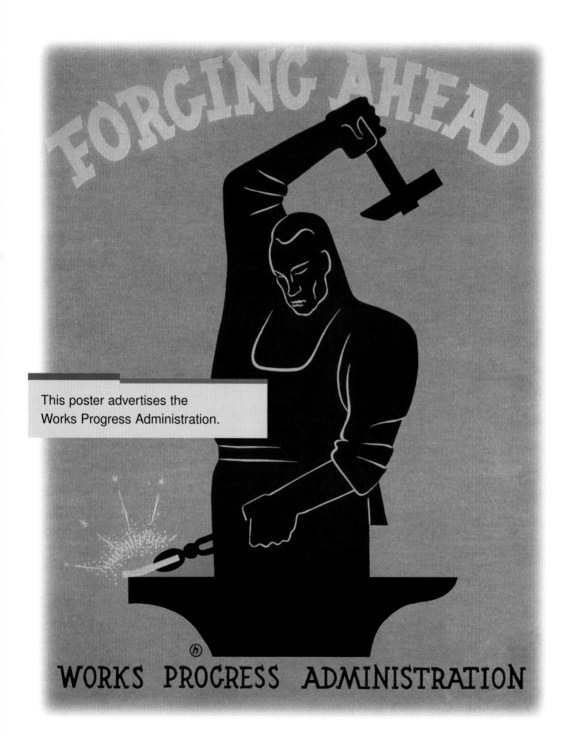

This poster advertises the Works Progress Administration.

policy of open books would prevent stocks from being overvalued as they were in 1929.

New Deal measures continued to aid those Americans Roosevelt once called forgotten men. The Works Progress Administration (WPA) was founded in late 1933. The WPA spent billions building bridges, highways, and sewage systems. These tasks were taken on as much to provide jobs as well as to produce useful results.

To help working people buy houses, Congress passed legislation to create the Federal Housing Administration (FHA) in 1934. The FHA guaranteed repayment of loans a homeowner owed to a bank. For example, working people frequently lost their jobs during the depression. Unemployed men and women could not meet their monthly mortgage payments to the banks. In such cases the FHA made the mortgage payment. That way the unemployed workers were allowed to keep their homes.

The rights of working people to form labor unions was addressed by the New Deal. For years, bosses were free to fire

Robert Wagner, Champion of Labor

The National Labor Relations Act was introduced by Senator Robert Ferdinand Wagner of New York. The measure is often called the Wagner Act. Robert Wagner (1877–1953) was born in Germany. He immigrated to the United States with his family when he was eight years old. As a powerful Democratic senator, Wagner was a crusader for the rights of workers. Though a Roosevelt supporter, he often went further than the president wished when creating prolabor legislation. Wagner introduced the Social Security Act and the U.S. Housing Act of 1937. His son, Robert F. Wagner, served as mayor of New York City from 1954 to 1965.

workers who tried to organize unions. The National Labor Relations Act of 1935 gave federal-government protection to unions. The act created the National Labor Relations Board (NLRB). This agency confirmed the rights of workers to form unions and to bargain with their bosses over wages and working conditions. The NLRB served as sort of a labor court. Workers took their grievances to board members of the NLRB and asked for rulings.

Many projects built by a New Deal agency had a special marker. This marker appears on a sidewalk that was built by the Works Progress Administration in Providence, Rhode Island.

The Social Security Act was passed in 1935. The act created the Social Security system. At first, Social Security gave cash payments to retired people who had worked in commerce or industry. In 1939, Social Security was expanded to cover the wives and children of retired workers. Over the years, Social Security benefits continued to expand. In 1965, Congress passed Medicare, which provides health insurance for people over age sixty-five. Social Security is a safety net, an insurance program that protects people from the extremes of poverty. Today, every working American contributes to Social Security. No other New Deal law has had such a long-standing impact on American life.[7]

The high cost of the New Deal frightened many people. The Federal Relief Appropriations Act, which included the WPA, began with a $5 billion budget, then the greatest single appropriation ever. To finance the New Deal, the government fell into debt. Americans worried because the government was spending money it did not have. They feared that this policy of government or national debt could lead to financial disaster.

The Roosevelt Brain Trust reasoned that spending money—even though it was borrowed money—would recharge the economy. They called this operation "priming the pump." Most people of the time readily understood that term. Water in the 1930s was often drawn from a backyard well using a hand pump. Pouring a can of water over the moving parts swelled the pump's rubber gaskets and hastened the action of getting water out of the spout. This dousing was called priming the pump. So, it was reasoned, government money injected into the economy primed the circulation of money and encouraged private funds to flow freely through the country once more.

The New Deal At Work

I can remember the first week of the CWA checks. It was on a Friday. That night everybody had gotten his check. The first check a lot of them had in three years. . . . I never saw such a change in attitude. Instead of walking around and feeling dreary and looking sorrowful, everybody was joyous. . . . If Roosevelt had run for President the next day, he'd have gone in by a hundred percent.[1]

Hank Oettinger, a Chicagoan who recalled the joy he and fellow workers felt after getting their first paychecks from the Civil Works Administration (CWA), a New Deal agency.

The TVA: Miracle in the Marsh

A lush forest covered the Tennessee River Valley when colonists moved to the region in the 1700s. Immediately, the colonists began cutting down the trees to establish farms. Without tree roots to hold the ground in place the rich topsoil washed into the river. Over the years, farming in the valley became virtually impossible. In winter, when heavy rains came, the river flooded. The Tennessee Valley, once a magnificent forest, became a dismal swamp.

In the early 1900s, the Tennessee Valley was perhaps the nation's most impoverished region. Families lived in shacks with no running water or electricity. Average family income was about one hundred dollars a year. Torrential rains regularly turned the Tennessee River into a raging killer. Floods took hundreds of lives and made thousands of people homeless.

The Tennessee Valley Authority (TVA) was designed to correct problems created by human activity. In one of the largest construction projects ever attempted in the United States, TVA engineers set out to build a series of dams designed to control the Tennessee River. Moreover, the TVA was a broad regional authority whose works and projects crossed state lines. The river and its branches flowed through parts of Kentucky, Virginia, North Carolina, Georgia, Alabama, and Mississippi. In all, the valley spread over some forty thousand square miles.

Beginning in 1933, crews constructed thirty-five dams along the Tennessee River and its many tributaries. Water gathered behind the dams during the rainy winter months and was released gradually in the drier summer period. This practice kept the river at a consistent level and prevented flooding. Flowing water also drove turbines to generate electricity. The

A carpenter works on the Douglas Dam, a TVA project.

dams made the once-wild river navigable for large cargo boat traffic.

Taking a revolutionary step, the TVA established a government agency to provide electrical power to paying customers. This broke precedent in America where electricity was traditionally distributed by private power companies. Government-supplied power was the vision of George William Norris (1861–1944), a senator from Nebraska. Norris was a Republican. Most Republicans believed in leaving electrical generators in the hands of private industry. But Norris argued that private companies would never attempt to harness the Tennessee River because the costs were too great and the profits uncertain. True to his dream, Norris introduced legislation that created the TVA. Soon, electricity supplied by TVA generators provided lighting for 50 million homes. One of the project's largest dams, the Norris Dam, is named after the visionary senator from Nebraska.

Initially, the TVA met resistance from those it was designed to help most—the impoverished farmers of the region. The Tennessee hillfolk were a proud people. They were leery of outsiders who wanted to impose changes in their lives. Many Tennessee families would have to move to create room for the dams and their reservoirs. Even centuries-old graveyards needed to be dug up and relocated. The people finally accepted the TVA because of the promise of jobs. Local men were hired immediately to clear land for the dams.

The Norris Dam, as it appears today

By June 1934, in the TVA's first full year of construction, 9,173 people worked for the agency.[2] Their average pay was about $45 a week, a high salary by depression standards. Thousands of women were also hired by the TVA. Women earned the same as men when they worked the same jobs. However, women were not put to work as construction laborers. Instead, female TVA employees were assigned to be cooks and office clerks. The jobs given to women usually paid less than work performed by men toiling on construction projects.

As the series of dams neared completion, the once-impoverished Tennessee Valley glowed with new life. Flood control allowed new farms to be established. Factories appeared where factories had never operated before. Many new factories there produced fertilizers to aid farmers around the nation. Fueling this revitalized Tennessee Valley was an abundance of electrical power. Generators operated by the TVA supplied electricity for power and light to eighty-three government-owned power companies.[3] The companies sold the power to customers at affordable prices. Electricity had come to the rural Tennessee Valley region for the first time.

Jobs, Boondoggles, and the WPA

People of the 1930s took pride in their work. Living on public assistance was considered a shameful practice. It was generally believed that only lazy people asked for a government hand-out. Yet the depression forced desperate people into the welfare offices. The mayor of Toledo, Ohio, said, "I have seen thousands of these defeated, discouraged, hopeless men and women, cringing and fawning as they come to ask for public aid. It is a spectacle of national degeneration."[4]

Ben Isaacs once owned a clothing store in Chicago. Isaacs lost his business during the depression. He could not find a job even though he walked the streets ten hours a day looking for work. "I didn't want to go on relief," Isaacs remembered years later. "Believe me, when I was forced to go to the office of the relief, the tears were running out of my eyes. . . . If it wasn't for [my] kids—I tell you the truth—many a time it came to my mind to go commit suicide."[5]

The Works Progress Administration (WPA) offered a paycheck for honest work instead of a relief payment.

The WPA was headed by Harry Hopkins, a powerful member of Roosevelt's New Deal staff. Hopkins understood the frustrations felt by working fathers struggling to support families in those hard times. His policy was to give a man a job, any sort of a job, and preserve his pride.

WPA crews built highways, bridges, schools, and municipal buildings such as city halls. Sometimes the agency sponsored projects for which there was no immediate need. For example, WPA laborers laid sidewalks in the far reaches of cities where no houses had yet been built. Anti-Roosevelt politicians called this make-work, an empty effort to invent jobs. However, job creation was the primary mission of the WPA. The usefulness of the agency's projects could be debated later.

Of all the New Deal agencies, the WPA generated the most controversy. Opponents said the WPA engaged in boondoggles, or useless activities which wasted time and money. Much of this criticism was due to Harry Hopkins' insistence that all sectors of American society be given jobs under the WPA umbrella. Thus, artists were put to work creating murals (wall paintings) in and on public buildings. Writers were assigned to write articles and stories about American life. Community theaters were created to give jobs to actors and directors. WPA orchestras and dance groups performed before enthusiastic audiences. Critics cried that the projects were boondoggles.

This mural, called "History of Southern Illinois" was painted by Paul Kelpe, as part of the WPA Illinois Federal Art Project.

Hopkins snapped back, "Hell they've [the writers and artists] got to eat just like other people."[6]

One writer who held a job with the WPA was John Steinbeck (1902–1968). His WPA assignment was certainly labeled a boondoggle by critics. In the early 1930s, Steinbeck was told to take a census of all dogs on California's Monterey Peninsula. He did his job, collected his paychecks, and survived the leanest period of the Great Depression. And he kept writing. Steinbeck produced masterpieces such as *Of Mice and Men* (1937) and *East of Eden* (1952). His epic novel *The Grapes Of Wrath* (1939) told the compelling story of an American family struggling to survive the Great Depression.

African Americans benefited from the WPA. Long before the Great Depression, African Americans complained they were the last hired and first fired. Under WPA rules, blacks earned the same as whites and they enjoyed job security. For many African Americans,

The American Guide Series

In older, long-established libraries you might still find a collection of worn-looking books written by WPA authors. They described all the states and some of the larger cities. Their titles were *The WPA Guide to Illinois*, *The WPA Guide to California*, and so on. The material contained in the books is now dated, but they remain fascinating reading because of the timeless stories they tell. Featured in the WPA guidebooks are tours the authors give of small towns. They bring the character of the town to life by describing the owner of a particular general store or the personality of a local preacher.

Your own town is likely covered in the guidebooks. It is fun to read this material to get the feel of town life as it was lived long ago. Here is a typical description of the town of Galena, Illinois, written in 1939 in the book *The WPA Guide to Illinois*: "Its [Galena's] streets climb tortuously from level to level of the ancient river bed, and the houses cling to the hills like chalets in an Alpine village."[7]

This poster advertises the *WPA Guide to California*.

this equal treatment in the 1930s seemed nothing short of a miracle. One African-American WPA laborer from North Carolina said, "The gover'ment is the best boss I ever had."[8] Richard Wright (1908–1960) was an unemployed African-American writer who helped compile *The WPA Guide to Harlem*. Wright went on to become one of the most influential writers of his time with books such as *Native Son* (1940) and *Black Boy* (1945).

Even in its peak year of 1938, the WPA employed only 405,700 women, about 13.5 percent of its total workforce.[9] Often, women were relegated to sewing projects, recreation supervision, and cooking in school lunch programs. These domestic-type jobs again paid far less than construction work on the WPA payroll. Ellen Woodward, a high-ranking officer in the WPA, tried to get the agency to expand its women's programs. However, women were still denied high-paying jobs within the agency. Men were thought of as the family breadwinners in the 1930s. Even Roosevelt believed the WPA should give preference to unemployed men first.

The WPA was the biggest of all New Deal agencies. In its eight-year lifetime, the WPA employed 8.5 million men and women.[10] WPA crews constructed 651,087 miles of highways; they built or repaired 124,031 bridges; and they erected 125,110 public buildings.[11] Some WPA buildings were architectural masterpieces. The Timberline Lodge on Oregon's Mount Hood and the Dock Street Theater in Charleston, South Carolina, were WPA creations. WPA crews built anything, even a new monkey cage for the Oklahoma City zoo. The Federal Music Project, part of the WPA, employed 15,000 musicians and gave 225,000 performances.[12] Many concerts were presented free to the public in city parks.

Though the WPA was attacked by Roosevelt's critics, it was loved by most of its employees. In 1936, a group of WPA workers from Battle Creek, Michigan, wrote a joint letter to Franklin Roosevelt and implored, "Please continue this W.P.A. program. It makes us feel like an American citizen to earn our own living."[13] Still another satisfied WPA working man composed a poem to his president and sent it to the White House:

> *I THINK THAT WE SHALL NEVER SEE*
> A PRESIDENT LIKE UNTO THEE . . .
> POEMS ARE MADE BY FOOLS LIKE ME,
> BUT GOD, I THINK, MADE FRANKLIN D.[14]

Alphabet Soup and American Life

Dozens of depression-era programs touched the everyday lives of Americans. The programs were usually called by their initials. Thus Americans lived under the spell of alphabet soup.

The Civilian Conservation Corps (CCC) was one of the most popular agencies of the time. The CCC took unemployed young men, ages seventeen through twenty-four, off the city streets and put them to work in the forests. Many of the young men were from city slums. They lived in camps and experienced the wonders of nature for the first time. For most, it was an unforgettable chapter in their lives. A man named Blackie Gold served in CCC camps in Michigan and Idaho. Years later, Gold told writer Studs Terkel, "I really enjoyed it. I had three wonderful square meals a day . . . They sure made a man out of ya."[15]

From 1933 to 1942, the year the agency closed, the CCC employed more than three million young men.[16] They slept in tents which were borrowed from the army. Military rules prevailed: They had to line up for roll call and inspection each morning. Camp supervisors were often World War I veterans. About 6 percent of the CCC's enrollment was made up of young African-American men.[17] But the African Americans were relegated to separate camps. The agency's director, Robert Fechner from Tennessee, insisted on racial segregation. All CCC members were paid thirty dollars a month. They were required to send twenty-five dollars each month home to their families. The youthful workers planted trees, built firewatch towers, and constructed hiking trails. They fought forest fires, erected log bridges, and cleared space for campgrounds and public beaches. Many of the magnificent log field houses which grace state and national parks today were constructed in the 1930s by boys and men of the CCC.

Another program dedicated to help young people was the National Youth Administration (NYA). Over the course of seven years, the NYA gave part-time jobs to some six hundred thousand college students and 1.5

Members of the CCC
move logs in a forest.

million high schoolers. Young people not attending
school were given training programs to let them
become stonemasons, carpenters, and professional
cooks. In 1935, the NYA director in Texas was a man
named Lyndon Johnson. He resigned from the agency
when he won a seat in Congress. (Johnson later became
the thirty-sixth president of the United States in 1963.)

Life on the nation's farms improved under the New
Deal. The Rural Electrification Administration (REA)
gave loans to private power firms. The REA required the
companies to string lines to isolated farming communities. In 1935, when the REA was born, only one in ten
American farms had electricity. Fifteen years later, nine

in ten farms had power. Many farmers were able to buy new tractors or build a modern barn through loans they received from the Farm Security Administration (FSA).

During the Great Depression, American farmers were frequently forced to sell their land. Farmers who owed money to banks could raise cash only through the sale of their holdings. These forced sales enraged farming communities. Angry farmers sometimes threatened to beat up or shoot the bankers who took over a neighbor's farm. The Farm Credit Administration (FCA) gave loans to farmers who were facing bankruptcy. Aid from the FCA saved many family farms, and brought peace to the rural regions.

Low prices for farm products plagued farmers throughout the 1930s. The Agricultural Adjustment Act (AAA) of 1933 attempted to raise prices by withholding farm goods from the market. The AAA paid farmers not to grow crops and to destroy or "plow under" crops that were ready for harvest. In 1933, cotton farmers were paid to plow under thousands of acres of cotton. The next year, the price for raw cotton almost doubled. Cotton was used in making clothing, and destroying it raised few complaints. But withholding food from a hungry nation was another matter entirely. When the AAA ordered farmers to destroy millions of pigs and throw away the meat, jobless people in cities protested. They thought this was a waste of food that could have been provided to them.

The New Deal attempted to elevate life for low-paid

factory workers. In 1938, Congress passed the Fair Labor Standards Act (FLSA). The act required employers to pay a minimum wage of 25 cents an hour to all workers and it set the maximum workweek at forty-four hours. The FLSA also prohibited children under sixteen from working in factories during school hours. These measures—a minimum wage, a maximum workweek, and a ban on child labor—were reforms that labor leaders had been demanding for decades.

Prices and Wages by 1930s Standards

A minimum wage of 25 cents an hour translated to a weekly paycheck of only $11. This pay scale seems absurdly low by today's standards, but goods were far cheaper in the 1930s:

Item	Cost
Women's cloth coat	$6.98
Men's overcoat	$11.00
Sled for a child	$1.45
Bicycle	$10.95
Baseball glove and ball	$1.25
Pound of bacon	$0.22
Quart of milk	$0.10
Dozen eggs	$0.29
Dodge automobile (new)	$595.00
Ford 1929 automobile (used)	$57.50[18]

The New Deal and the Lingering Depression

Roosevelt gave us quite a bit of hope, early. He probably saved us from complete collapse, in that sense. But he did not answer the things [about pulling us out of the Great Depression] . . . Because we had never been in anything like this [before].[1]

—David Kennedy, an economist who worked for the Roosevelt Administration during the Great Depression. In the 1970s, Kennedy served as secretary of the treasury under President Richard Nixon.

Private Industry: Sluggishness and Strife

Jobs increased in the early New Deal years, but by 1934 more than 11 million people remained out of work. In fact, despite the New Deal measures, unemployment figures remained high throughout the 1930s.

Unemployment Year-by-Year in the 1930s

Year	Workforce Unemployed
1930	8.9%
1931	15.9%
1932	23.6%
1933	24.9%
1934	21.7%
1935	20.1%
1936	17.0%
1937	14.3%
1938	19.0%
1939	17.2%[2]

The New Deal was a public (government-sponsored) program. However, the vast majority of the nation's jobs were generated by the private (nongovernment) sector. In the past, industries such as steel and manufacturing hired the bulk of workers in the private sector. Through much of the 1930s, those firms remained mired in the mud of the Great Depression. Americans who held jobs feared they could be fired with little or no notice. Because they had no job security, people hesitated to spend money on automobiles, refrigerators, and other manufactured goods. This meant factories producing such consumer goods operated at far less than full capacity. By 1936, the nation's total industrial production still had not reached 1929 figures.

Factory work, even before the Great Depression, was grueling. Men and women on assembly lines toiled at exhausting speeds. Machine operators were required to produce so many pieces per hour or lose their jobs. Labor unions promised to improve working conditions. Factory owners branded union organizers as troublemakers or even communists. Anger erupted in the workplace. Many middle-class people feared a communist revolution would take place in the United States.

Workers who urged fellow employees to join unions were often dismissed. Because everyone feared a job loss, industrial workers mostly rejected the union message at first. As the Great Depression dragged on, however, underpaid factory hands began to defy their bosses and listen to labor leaders. Also, New Deal agencies such as the National Labor Relations Board (NLRB) guaranteed some protection of union rights. Under NLRB rules, it was illegal to fire a person for union activity. Between 1933 and 1935, union membership increased by one million.

Led by unions, a series of labor strikes rocked the private sector. Strikes hit the textile and auto industries. Truck drivers in Minnesota walked off their jobs and tied up transport in a dozen northern states. What began as a strike by San Francisco longshoremen in 1934 grew into a general strike supported by thousands. Much of San Francisco was shut down. Even the city's tailors, gas station attendants, and barbers refused to work.

Most strikes of the early 1930s failed to bring workers higher wages and better conditions. Even though business owners were losing money during the Great Depression, still they generally had enough funds to wait out strikes. Workers had families to feed and could not survive without their weekly paycheck. Therefore strikes tended to fizzle before the working people achieved their goals. Out of desperation, workers turned to novel and sometimes violent tactics in their battle against the captains of industry.

In December 1936, men and women of the General Motors (GM) plant in Flint, Michigan, reported to their jobs as usual. Once inside the factory building, they sat at their machines. The GM employees refused to work, and they refused to leave the plant. The auto assemblers of Flint launched the nation's first major "sit-down strike." For six weeks the workers remained locked in the GM plant. Family members brought them meals by passing pots and dishes through the factory windows. Police were summoned. The workers threw nuts, bolts, and coffee mugs at the officers and chased them out of the building. The sit-down tactic completely shut down the auto plant. Finally, GM officials agreed to negotiate and the workers won new rights.

Other sit-down strikes were waged in American factories with varying results. The Supreme Court finally declared sit-down strikes to be illegal because they amounted to a takeover of private property. Yet the sit-down movement captured the spirit of frustrated workers. The strikes were a unique way to show labor's defiance of capital. Sit-down strikers often chanted these words:

> *When the boss won't talk, don't take a walk.*
> *Sit down! Sit down!*[3]

The Republic Steel plant on Chicago's South Side

Union members stage a sit-down strike at the General Motors Fisher Body Plant in Flint, Michigan.

employed thousands of people. The employees formed a union, but the bosses refused to deal with the union organization. On Memorial Day 1937, the workers and their families held a rally outside the plant. Chicago police ordered them to leave. Union leaders said they had a right to demonstrate. A police captain accused the workers of being communists. Someone threw a tree branch at the police who then opened fire on the crowd. In minutes, ten people were shot dead and thirty were wounded.[4] The battle at Republic Steel was the bloodiest labor clash of the depression era.

Years later, the steelworkers' union took its case to the National Labor Relations Board (NLRB) and won major concessions. However, no government agency could ease the pain of the families who lost loved ones on Memorial Day 1937.

The Dust Bowl, Nightmare of the Great Depression

For years a drought plagued the midwestern section of the United States. Also, too many ranches and farms operated in the region. Grazing cattle had chewed the grasses into stubs. The thinned-out grass was unable to hold the topsoil in place.

Early one November morning in 1933, an eerie black cloud appeared over the wheat fields of South Dakota. "By mid-morning a gale was blowing, cold and black," said a *Saturday Evening Post* writer. "By noon it was blacker than night. . . . It was a wall of dirt one's eyes could not penetrate, but it could penetrate the eyes and ears and nose. It could penetrate to the lungs until one coughed up blood."[5]

This was the start of the Dust Bowl. A lack of rain and overgrazing turned much of the midwest into a virtual desert. Winds swept into the region creating a storm of dust unlike anything ever seen before. It was a cruel, double blow for people already suffering due to the Great Depression. The Dust Bowl area ran from Texas to the Canadian border. Cars had to drive with lights on even in the middle of the day. Once-productive farms became covered with drifting sand and soil.

Rural people in the Dust Bowl area were forced to move and seek work. Most headed to California riding in battered cars and trucks. The migrating farmers were called the "Okies," short for Oklahoma, although they came from at least a dozen states. Hungry and homeless, the Dust Bowl fugitives made up a sad parade. Their plight was powerfully portrayed in John Steinbeck's novel *The Grapes of Wrath*:

> And the migrants streamed in on the highways and their hunger was in their eyes, and their need was in their eyes. They had no argument, no system, nothing but their numbers and their needs. When there was work for a man, ten men fought for it—fought with a low wage. If that fella'll work for thirty cents, I'll work for twenty-five. If he'll take twenty five, I'll do it for twenty. No, me I'm hungry. I'll work for fifteen. I'll work for food.[6]

The Demagogues

As the stubborn depression continued, Roosevelt and the New Deal came under attack from the right and from the left. From the right were the conservatives, including the Republicans, who resisted all change. From the left stood the liberals, including Democrats, Progressives, Communists, and others, who complained the changes brought about by the New Deal were too few and too slow.

Three men—Huey Long, Dr. Francis Townsend, and Father Charles E. Coughlin—rose to prominence as critics of the government during the depression.

None of the three had ties to left-wing or right-wing movements. They were demagogues, leaders who seek power and influence by appealing to the passions of the masses.

Huey Long was a pudgy man with bright red hair. He wore flashy clothes and his roaring laugh could be heard across a crowded room. Long was born in a poor farm community in Louisiana. He rose from his humble status and was elected Louisiana's governor in 1928 and its senator in 1930. Long was a Democrat and, at first, a Roosevelt supporter. As the depression lingered, Long proposed radical ways to end the slump. In fiery speeches he demanded the government provide all families with a house, an automobile, a radio, and an income of five thousand dollars a year. Long gave vague answers when asked where money for these items would come from. Masses of poor people adored Long. The Democrats feared he would split their party by running for president in 1936. Long was shot and killed in September 1935 by Carl A. Weiss. The Weiss family were longtime enemies of Huey Long.

Another scheme for ending the depression came from a California doctor named Francis Townsend. The doctor advanced the Townsend Plan, which would give a pension of two hundred dollars a month to every American over the age of sixty. This proposed grant was considerably higher than monthly Social Security payments. Elderly people receiving the money would be required to spend the full sum. In this way, the funds spent by older people would stimulate the economy. Townsend called for a tax on businesses to provide for the monthly pensions. The proposal drew wide interest. Townsend claimed to have 25 million followers, both young and old. Opponents said the Townsend Plan would bankrupt the government. A version of the plan reached Congress in 1939, but it was voted down. Townsend faded into history.

A popular depression-era speaker was Father Charles Coughlin, a Catholic priest from a Detroit, Michigan, suburb. He was sometimes called the Radio Priest. His regular radio show was heard by millions. Coughlin was a passionate foe of communism. He believed that communist ideas were growing stronger because of the depression. He blamed the depression on Jewish bankers and Wall Street

Father Charles Coughlin makes a speech at 1938 convention.

stockbrokers. Often, Father Coughlin attacked Roosevelt and the New Deal. His speeches also became increasingly anti-Semitic (anti-Jewish). Finally, his superiors in the Catholic Church ordered Coughlin to stop doing radio shows. Father Coughlin obeyed and quietly returned to his parish in Michigan.

The 1936 Election: The People Approve the New Deal

In 1936, the Democrats nominated Franklin Roosevelt for a second term. On the campaign trail, the president claimed the New Deal was providing relief for poor people and pushing the economy forward. Often, he asked Americans to think back to the early years of the Great Depression when the economic picture looked miserable. In Chicago, on October 14, 1936, Roosevelt said the New Deal benefited business owners as well as workers:

> Today for the first time in seven years the banker, the store-keeper, the small factory owner, the industrialist, can all sit back and enjoy the company of their own ledgers. They are in the black [showing a profit]. That is where we want them to be; that is where our policies aim that they shall be; that is where we intend them to be in the days to come.[7]

This button was used during Roosevelt's 1936 campaign for reelection.

The Republicans picked Alfred Landon, the governor of Kansas, as their candidate for president. Landon was a mild-mannered politician who admitted that certain aspects of the New Deal had benefited the country. But Landon continually pointed out that

Roosevelt's programs were driving the United States deeply into debt and still leaving millions of people unemployed. Landon and the Republicans enjoyed the support of most of the nation's newspapers. Bankers and industrial leaders also backed the Republican candidate.

On November 3, 1936, the nation voted. Roosevelt and the Democrats won in one of the most lopsided votes ever recorded. Landon carried only Maine and Vermont. The other forty-six states went to Roosevelt. The Democrats increased their majority in both the House of Representatives and the Senate. Roosevelt supporters proudly sang a victory song:

> We've got Franklin D. Roosevelt back again.
> We'll have money in our jeans,
> We can travel with the queen,
> We've got Franklin D. Roosevelt back again.[8]

The New Deal Versus the Supreme Court

The 1936 vote demonstrated Roosevelt's popularity with the people. However, his New Deal program faced serious opposition from the United States Supreme Court.

The Supreme Court can overturn an act of Congress if the justices believe the act violates the Constitution. This role of the Supreme Court is part of a concept called the separation of powers. The Constitution divides government into three branches or powers: the President (the executive branch), the Congress (the legislative branch), and the Supreme

Roosevelt's Second Inaugural Address

President Roosevelt delivered his second inaugural speech on January 20, 1937. It was one of his most famous speeches. For the most part it had an optimistic tone. But the address reminded the audience that many Americans still suffered due to the Great Depression:

> But here is the challenge to our democracy: In this nation I see tens of millions of its citizens—a substantial part of its whole population—who at this very moment are denied the greater part of what the very lowest standards of today call the necessities of life.
>
> I see millions of families trying to live on incomes so meager that the pall of family disaster hangs over them day by day.
>
> I see millions denied education, recreation, and then opportunity to better their lot and the lot of their children.
>
> I see millions lacking the means to buy the products of farm and factory and by their poverty denying work and productiveness to other many millions.
>
> I see one-third of a nation ill-housed, ill-clad, ill-nourished.
>
> It is not in despair that I paint you that picture. I paint it for you in hope—because the Nation, seeing and understanding the injustice in it, proposes to paint it out.[9]

Court (the judicial branch). In theory, each of the three powers serves as a watchdog over the others. In this way, no single branch can assume undue authority.

As early as 1935, the Supreme Court struck down a provision of the National Industrial Recovery Act because it gave lawmaking powers to a government agency. The Court claimed lawmaking authority ought to rest with the legislative branch. Later, the Court declared the Agricultural Adjustment Act and several other New Deal measures unconstitutional.

Roosevelt fumed. He believed the Supreme Court was poised to strike down most if not all of his New Deal legislation. In February 1937, Roosevelt said he wanted to appoint additional justices to the Supreme Court. Clearly this move was designed to dilute, or weaken, the authority of older justices. Under the proposal, new justices would sit on the Court along with current members many of whom had reached the age of seventy. It was no coincidence that older justices on the Court generally were enemies of the New Deal. Roosevelt's proposal would allow him to expand the Supreme Court from nine justices to fifteen.

On March 9, 1937, Roosevelt addressed the nation by radio. The president spoke of his plan to change the makeup of the Supreme Court:

> We have, therefore, reached the point as a Nation where we must take action to save the Constitution from the Court and the Court from itself. . . . We want a Supreme Court which will do justice under the Constitution—not over it. In

our Courts we want a government of laws and
not of men.[10]

As usual, the president made an eloquent and powerful speech. But from every corner of the country,
Americans condemned what was called the "court-
packing" bill. On the surface, the president's
suggestion did not seem radical. The Constitution does
not say how many justices should sit on the bench of
the Supreme Court. The number of justices has varied.
But the public feared Roosevelt's intent. The court-
packing act would allow a president to add justices
every time he had a disagreement with the Supreme
Court. He would naturally have picked justices that
agreed with his politics. This would destroy the historic concept of separation of powers by severely
weakening the judicial branch. Even FDR's friends in
Congress refused to back him on this proposal.
Roosevelt was accused of wanting to become a dictator.
Some Americans claimed the president had gone mad.
A woman from South Carolina, alarmed about the
Court plan, wrote her senator, "Don't, don't let that
wild man in the White House do this dreadful thing to
our country."[11]

In July 1937, a version of the court reform bill went
to the Senate. It was defeated by a vote of 70 to 20.
Roosevelt had lost. Opposition to tampering with the
system of separation of powers was just too great.
However, in time, the justices began approving New Deal
measures. Also, older justices resigned. This allowed
FDR to appoint new men whom he believed would be

more on his side. Despite all this, the court-packing conflict with the Court left deep scars on the Roosevelt image.

"Don't, don't let that wild man in the White House do this dreadful thing to our country."

—A women in South Carolina concerned over Roosevelt's court-packing plan.

The Roosevelt Recession

In the fall of 1937, another business slowdown struck the American economy. Problems started, familiarly, when stock prices dropped. Fearful of another stock market disaster, companies laid off workers. In the second half of 1937, some 2 million Americans lost their jobs. Payrolls around the country fell 35 percent.

The term recession was new in 1937. A recession is an economic blow not as severe as a depression. A very disappointed President Roosevelt admitted the reversal and said, "It makes no difference to me whether you call it a recession or a depression."[12] Critics blamed the problem on the president and called it the Roosevelt Recession.

Ironically, the recession was worsened even more by Roosevelt's sudden unwillingness to spend government money. Despite what his enemies said, the president feared debt. In the darkest days of the Great Depression, FDR encouraged debt in order to prime the pump and get money flowing through the economy.

Jobs in the 1930s

Creating jobs was the major goal of the New Deal. Jobs in the 1930s paid a fraction of what they do today. For example, a public schoolteacher in 1934 earned a little more than $1,200 a year. Today, a beginning teacher in a big-city system has an annual salary of about $35,000. Here is a list of jobs and typical pay scales for workers in the 1930s:

Bus driver	$1,373
College teacher	$3,111
Construction worker	$907
Dentist	$2,391
Doctor	$3,382
Dressmaker	$780
Lawyer	$4,218
Priest	$831
Railroad conductor	$2,729
Secretary	$1,040
Waitress	$520[13]

However, by 1937 the President decided that the worst of the depression was over. Private industry was hiring workers. Tax money flowed into the government treasury. Roosevelt decided it was a good opportunity to cut government spending.

In early 1937, the president reduced spending on relief programs. Then came the sudden stock market decline which frightened the business community. By the end of 1937, two in every ten workers were unemployed. The jobless rate remained high for the rest of the 1930s. In fact, not until 1941 did unemployment fall below 10 percent.

The recession of 1937 hurt the president politically. Many observers said the recession stood as proof the New Deal had failed. Republicans began teaming up with Southern Democrats to form a new coalition opposed to Roosevelt's policies. But the American people, who believed their lives were saved by programs such as the WPA and the TVA, remained loyal to the president. FDR won two more terms in the White House in 1940 and 1944. No president in American history was as successful on election days as was Franklin Roosevelt.

The New Dealers

Years later after the Social Security Act was passed, I saw how it worked in individual cases in this area. There was a mine accident in which several men were killed, and my husband asked me to go down and find out what the people were saying. . . . I asked [one woman who had lost her husband] how she was going to manage. She seemed quite confident and told me: "My sister and her two children will come to live with us. I am going to get Social Security benefits of nearly sixty-five dollars a month. I pay fifteen dollars a month on my house and land, and I shall raise vegetables and have chickens and with the money from the government I will get along very well."[1]

Eleanor Roosevelt, from her book *This I Remember*. The first lady was a prominent New Dealer, one of many men and women who supported New Deal programs and made them work.

Who Were the New Dealers?

To run the New Deal, Roosevelt brought to Washington people with fine minds and determined personalities. New Dealers came from businesses, college campuses, law firms, engineering companies, and the military.

Most, but certainly not all, were Democrats. Many New Dealers were themselves wealthy. A small, but surprising, number of the president's New Dealers were women. This was unusual in the 1930s when women rarely served as bosses over men.

New Dealers understood that they were engaged in a unique mission. Attempting to improve the economy through massive public works was a concept never tried before in the United States. Roosevelt asked the New Dealers to ignore old rules and to treat the depression as

The Hollywood Dream Factory

Certainly the hard times of the 1930s gnawed at everyone's mind. But rarely did the movies of the period even mention the word "depression." Instead, moviemakers offered their customers fantasies, comedies, and high adventures. Average Americans, seeking escape from the harsh realities of their lives, went to the movies for pure entertainment.

Although Americans stayed away from movie theaters in the early to mid-1930s because of financial concerns, they were packing the seats again by the end of the decade. The 1937 Walt Disney animated film *Snow White and the Seven Dwarfs* drew a huge audience, perhaps because it told a happy story. Another favorite was *The Wizard of Oz* which portrayed the heroine Dorothy's journey through a fantastic land. More people saw the 1939 Civil War epic *Gone With The Wind*, which was filmed in blazing color, than any other movie made at that time. Around the country, more than fifteen thousand movie houses catered to the public. During the 1930s, some 60 percent of Americans went to the movies at least once a week.

a national emergency which required urgent measures. He hoped the New Dealers would rise up and recognize their unique place in history. In a 1936 speech, Roosevelt said, "There is a mysterious cycle in human events. To some generations much is given. Of other generations much is expected. This generation of Americans has a rendezvous with destiny."[2]

One prominent New Dealer was Hugh Johnson (1882–1942), a business executive and a former army general. Roosevelt put Johnson in charge of one of his favorite agencies, the National Recovery Administration (NRA). The NRA persuaded business owners to hire more workers and to give them fair wages. In this mission, Johnson confronted industry leaders and even bullied them. Millions of men and women were hired by NRA approved industrial firms. All was not perfect in the New Deal family, however. After the 1937 court-packing attempt, Hugh Johnson resigned from government and became a bitter enemy of Roosevelt and his policies.

Hugh Johnson was picked to be *Time* magazine's 1933 "Man of the Year" and appeared on a January 1, 1934 cover of the magazine.

Harold Ickes (1874–1952) was a successful lawyer and a Republican when Roosevelt brought him into the New Deal circle. Ickes headed the Public Works Administration (PWA). In this capacity, he controlled a $5 billion budget. His agency took on projects ranging from constructing enormous dams in the far west to erecting small town post office buildings in various parts of the nation. Ickes tolerated no mismanagement or dishonesty. Nicknamed Honest Harold, he carefully checked the financial figures of each project. Roosevelt, who demanded speed from his New Dealers, sometimes grew frustrated with Ickes. The PWA boss insisted on examining every detail before giving his go-ahead to a new project. Ickes also served as the United States secretary of the interior, a position he held from 1933 to 1946. Students still read Ickes's book *Diary*, which provides a fascinating history of his times.

Frances Perkins (1882–1965) was a schoolteacher and a social worker from Boston. In 1933, Roosevelt named her secretary of labor, making Perkins the first woman ever to serve in a cabinet position. She had the very tricky job of promoting workers' rights while trying to avoid stepping on the toes of business leaders. Her loyalty was with the workers. Perkins was a strong supporter of the Fair Labor Standards Act, which established a minimum wage and outlawed child labor. She also published a book, *The Roosevelt I Knew*, which is still read by scholars today.

Mary McLeod Bethune (1875–1955) was an important African-American New Dealer. Born in South

Secretary of Labor Frances Perkins shakes Roosevelt's hand in 1933.

Carolina to parents who were once enslaved, she founded Bethune-Cookman College, which educated African-American young women. A brilliant speaker, she traveled the country raising money for her college. In 1936, she was appointed a director in the New Deal's National Youth Administration (NYA). As an NYA administrator, Bethune continued her crusade to bring education and job training to African-American girls and women.

Another prominent African American was Robert C. Weaver (1907–1997). Born in Washington, Weaver was an economist who earned a doctoral degree from

Mary McLeod Bethune was president of Bethune-Cookman College until 1942. The college grew from a small school she started for African-American girls in 1904.

Harvard. He served in the New Deal with the U.S. Housing Authority. Weaver, Bethune, and other black Americans regularly met with FDR and advised the president on African-American affairs. In 1969, President Lyndon Johnson named Weaver the head of Housing and Urban Development, making him the nation's first African-American cabinet officer.

Harry Hopkins, King of the New Deal

Harry Hopkins (1890–1946) was one of FDR's closest friends and probably the most powerful New Dealer in Washington. Born in Iowa, Hopkins moved to New York as a young man and became a career social worker. He served as director of a boys camp and worked for the American Red Cross. In 1931, Franklin Roosevelt, then governor of New York, named Hopkins to head the state's Temporary Emergency Relief Administration. When Roosevelt moved to the White House, he took Hopkins with him. The new president appointed Hopkins head of the new Federal Emergency Relief Administration.

As chief of the nation's largest relief organization, Hopkins gave money to millions of poor people. However, doling out money was a task he intensely disliked. He believed people should work for pay. In the fall of 1933, FDR made him head of the Civil Works Administration (CWA), a job he took on with zeal and energy. In less than one month, he put four million men to work, and in four months he spent $933 million on various construction projects. In

Harry Hopkins sits at his desk in Washington, DC.

1935, FDR appointed him director of the WPA, the largest of the New Deal organizations. It was here Hopkins achieved his lasting fame. He regularly worked eighteen-hour days and traveled extensively to visit WPA construction projects.

In 1938, Hopkins became secretary of commerce. During World War II, he served as FDR's spokesman in meetings with Great Britain's Winston Churchill and the Soviet Union's Joseph Stalin. At one point, Hopkins actually lived in the White House. Rumors said Roosevelt was quietly grooming Hopkins to run for the presidency someday. But, handling an intense work schedule and smoking several packs of cigarettes a day, Hopkins was plagued by health problems. Harry Hopkins died on January 29, 1946, of stomach cancer.

Eleanor Roosevelt

The president's wife held no title in the New Deal, nor did she control an agency. Still, Eleanor Roosevelt exerted a powerful behind-the-scenes influence on the New Deal's direction. She was the most politically active first lady in American history.[3]

Eleanor Roosevelt (1884–1962) was born into the wealth and power of the Roosevelt family. Her childhood, however, was an unhappy one. Her mother, whom she feared, suffered from mental depression and died when Eleanor was eight years old. Her father, whom she adored, was an alcoholic who died two years after her mother. Eleanor led a lonely life in the care of her maternal grandmother. Her spirits improved at age fifteen when she was sent overseas to attend the Allenswood School near London. She emerged an attractive, intelligent young woman and the pride of the Roosevelt family. When she married Franklin in 1905, she was given away by her uncle, President Theodore Roosevelt.

Upon arriving in Washington, Eleanor Roosevelt established her own radio program. She also wrote a newspaper column called "My Day." Roosevelt put the money she made on this work to an interesting use: "With the first money I earned through commercial radio work, during the bad days of the depression, I established two places where girls who were unemployed and searching for work could have lunch and a place to rest."[4] This sort of direct involvement in social causes was a new role for a first lady. Previously, presidents'

"... I established two places where girls could have lunch and a place to rest."
—Eleanor Roosevelt on what she did with the money she earned from being on the radio.

wives were supposed to entertain White House guests and hold formal teas. Eleanor Roosevelt, like the New Deal itself, broke new ground.

The first lady worked tirelessly to increase the role of women and African Americans in the New Deal. However, the New Deal leadership remained predominantly white and male. Prejudice against African

Eleanor records a program called "My People" at a radio station in Washington, DC. The program was devoted to African Americans.

Americans was strong in the 1930s, and it was generally believed that women should be protected not promoted. The New Deal never reached Eleanor Roosevelt's goals of equality for women and African Americans. African Americans continued to live in separate facilities in TVA housing and in CCC camps. Women's work through the WPA was often limited to sewing projects.

However, Eleanor Roosevelt's efforts did pay off in some ways. It was largely due to her influence that the African-American educator Mary McLeod Bethune was promoted to be a director in the National Youth Administration. She also supported top female New Dealers such as Mary Dewson and Frances Perkins.

Eleanor Roosevelt frequently traveled alone on fact-finding tours to determine the progress of New Deal activity and make reports back to the president. Even those inspection trips stirred controversy. At the time, many people, including many women, thought it was undignified for a woman to tour construction sites in the company of male engineers and workers. But Eleanor Roosevelt continued to defy conventions. Promoting the New Deal became her duty as first lady. She once said, "I always looked at everything from the point of view of what I *ought* to do, rarely from what I wanted to do."[5]

The Twilight and End of the New Deal

. . . you have asked of us only one thing: that our job be well and truly done for the good of the Nation.[1]

—From a plaque given to Harold Ickes by departing PWA workers. The plaque was presented to Ickes on June 26, 1939, when the PWA was, in effect, officially dissolved.

The New Deal Fades Away

The New Deal began in March 1933, the day after Roosevelt's stirring inaugural address. On that cold March morning the president launched his depression-fighting agenda with a blizzard of laws passed during the First 100 Days. But while the New Deal had a definite and dramatic beginning, its ending date is less certain. It never officially ended. Instead, Congress refused to fund its programs and the once powerful agencies vanished one by one.

fascism, a political movement that swept Europe and other parts of the world in the 1920s and 1930s. Under fascism, a nation's industrial plants remain in private ownership but come under government control. Fascist governments call for extreme patriotism among their citizens, and they adopt a warlike stance toward neighboring states. Benito Mussolini brought fascism to Italy in 1922. In Spain, the fascist Francisco Franco rose to power in the late 1930s. A form of fascism also spread to Japan.

The Great Depression made extremist movements such as communism and fascism more acceptable in the minds of the masses. Poverty and a bleak feeling of hopelessness led even reasonable men and women to accept radical solutions to national problems. Fascism, which was always accompanied by militarism and dictatorship, grew stronger abroad as the depression lingered.

On September 1, 1939, Germany attacked Poland. That invasion marked the official start of World War II. For two years, America stayed out of the warfare raging in Europe. Then, on December 7, 1941, Japan attacked the American naval base at Pearl Harbor in Hawaii. The next day, Roosevelt announced that the United States was declaring war on Japan. Three days later, Germany, an ally of Japan, declared war on the United States. In the weeks following the attack on Pearl Harbor, more than fifty nations and half the world's population were caught up in the whirlwind of war.

In America, the demands of World War II sparked

The U.S.S. *California* emits thick clouds of black smoke as it sinks into Pearl Harbor after the Japanese attack.

the once sluggish economy. Jobs were suddenly abundant as the nation built ships, planes, and other tools for victory. By 1944, The American unemployment rate, which had been higher than 10 percent throughout the depression years, slipped to one percent of the workforce. But full employment prompted by warfare came with a heavy price. More than 1.2 million Americans were killed or wounded by the time the war ended in September 1945.

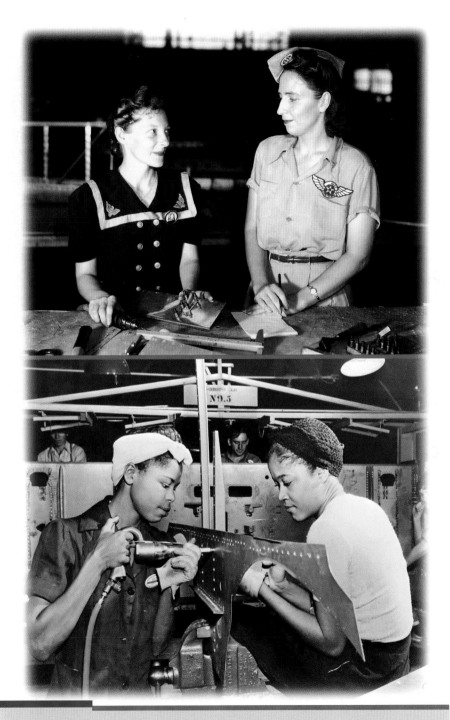

World War II opened new jobs for women. Top: These two widows of men killed at Pearl Harbor decided to work to help the war effort. Bottom: Here, two women help assemble airplanes at the Douglas Aircraft Company.

Lasting Projects Built by the PWA

There is confusion between the work of the PWA (Public Works Administration) and the WPA (Works Progress Administration) because their initials are similar and both were engaged in construction projects. Here are a few major accomplishments of the PWA that we enjoy today:

- All American Canal, an 80-mile-long canal that today brings water from the Colorado River to California's Imperial Valley and irrigates thousands of acres of farmland.

- The Gold Depository in Fort Knox, Kentucky, a solid thick-walled building that holds the nation's gold reserve.

- The Grand Coulee Dam, the nation's largest concrete dam, on the Columbia River near Spokane, Washington, provides electrical power for millions of households and irrigation for farms.

- The Lincoln Tunnel, an auto route that runs under the Hudson River and connects New York City to New Jersey, today serves thousands of daily commuters.

- The Mall in Washington, D.C., the broad, tree-lined plaza in the nation's capital, was improved by PWA workers and made into the pleasant walkway we know today.

- The Triborough Bridge, an engineering marvel, is actually a series of bridges which connect three New York City boroughs—Manhattan, the Bronx, and Queens.

A Look Back at the New Deal

Even in the twenty-first century, Americans enjoy the fruits of New Deal programs. The TVA continues to generate electricity which is used by millions. Social Security remains the prime retirement plan for older Americans. We still walk on sidewalks or drive over streets put down many years ago by WPA crews. Hundreds of schools, post office buildings, and public hospitals in use today were built by laborers earning $45 a month from a New Deal agency.

The New Deal gave the federal government a greater role in the lives of Americans. Before the Great Depression, when people spoke of "the government" they were most likely referring to their township or state government. In peacetime, at least, Americans had little contact with federal departments except for when they went to the post office to buy stamps. The New Deal changed that mindset. Suddenly federal government agencies, referred to by their initials, opened offices in small towns and city neighborhoods. The federal government now became "the government" in the minds of Americans.

Before the 1930s, families, churches, and local governments helped people in economic need. Then the Great Depression flooded the nation with poor men, women, and families. Only the federal government had the resources and funds to take care of the impoverished masses. In this respect the United States caught up with the industrial states of Europe. Central governments in Europe long had a tradition of providing

The TVA and the Atomic Bomb

The atomic bomb—the most destructive weapon ever created by humans—was developed by a supersecret program called the Manhattan Project. A major project facility was located in the town of Oak Ridge, Tennessee. Oak Ridge was once a lonely spot in the Tennessee Valley. During the war years, Oak Ridge grew into a city of fifty thousand people. Plants at Oak Ridge refined uranium, the atomic bomb's basic fuel. Making uranium required abundant electrical power. This power came from TVA generators, without which the war-ending bomb could not have been built.

individuals with services such as old-age pensions and health care. The New Deal put the United States on the road to provide many services that European powers did, with the notable exception of national healthcare.

A major question arises: Did the New Deal pull the country out of the Great Depression as Roosevelt intended it to do? In simple economic terms that answer would have to be "not entirely." Unemployment remained high. Poverty followed Americans like a grim shadow throughout the 1930s. People who lived through the Great Depression never forgot the suffering, the insecurity, and the gnawing hunger that they endured for ten long years. As one man told the writer Studs Terkel in 1970, "Survivors [of the depression] are still ridin' with the ghost—the ghost of those days when things came hard."[2]

Still, the New Deal gave the American people a fresh spirit. Launched at a time when many leaders feared food riots or even a communist revolution would break out, New Deal measures calmed the storm. Operating at speeds which were shocking for government officials, the newly-formed agencies hired millions of workers. No one earned more than bare-bones food and rent money, but they enjoyed a weekly paycheck. As the wife of one CWA worker proudly said, "We aren't on relief any more. My husband is working for the Government."[3]

The New Deal was often criticized as a government giveaway scheme that paid workers to loaf. In fact, incidents of loafing were rare. New Deal programs gave the people strength to struggle through the hard

The Gold Depository at Fort Knox was built by PWA workers in 1936. It houses more than $6 billion worth of gold.

times of the 1930s. That strength nurtured a spirit to win the terrible war of the 1940s. In her autobiography, Eleanor Roosevelt said:

> The old story of the men who leaned on their shovels and shirked was, of course, true here and there, but on the whole the United States can be proud of [the New Deal's] efforts. [It] pulled the country out of the depression and made it possible for us to fight the greatest and most expensive war in our history.[4]

1920 Franklin Delano Roosevelt (FDR) runs for vice president with the Democrat presidential candidate, James Cox; the Democrats lose, but Roosevelt establishes a national name.

1921 Stricken by polio, the thirty-nine-year-old FDR loses the use of his legs.

1926 Roosevelt is elected governor of New York.

1928 Amid the general prosperity of the 1920s, the Republican Herbert Hoover is elected president.

1929 In October, prices on the New York Stock Exchange suddenly drop, sending panic through the Wall Street community; the crash of 1929 marks the beginning of the Great Depression.

1931 Unemployment in the U.S. reaches 15.9 percent of the workforce.

1932 FDR is elected president.

1933 Immediately after taking office FDR launches the New Deal; in a flurry of activity called the First Hundred Days many new government agencies designed to fight the depression are created.

1934 Later New Deal measures such as the Federal Housing Administration (FHA) are passed.

1935 Congress approves the Social Security Act, the most important New Deal law, which still affects life in the U.S. today.

1936 FDR wins reelection by a huge majority of votes.

1937 President Roosevelt tries to weaken the Supreme Court by proposing a law which would allow him to appoint more justices to that body; another bad turn in the stock market creates what is called the "Roosevelt Recession."

1938 The last of the New Deal measures, the Fair Labor Standards Act, is passed.

1939 Germany invades Poland and World War II begins.

1941 Japan bombs the American naval base at Pearl Harbor, Hawaii, and the U.S. plunges into the war.

1945 Roosevelt dies on April 12; World War II officially ends on September 2 when Japan signs the terms of surrender.

Chapter One   Fear Itself

1. Harold Evans, *The American Century* (New York: Alfred A. Knopf, 1998), p. 241.

2. *The Annals of America, Volume 15: 1929–1939 The Great Depression* (Chicago and London: Encyclopaedia Britannica, Inc., 1976), p. 205.

3. Ibid.

4. Ibid., p. 208.

Chapter Two   The 1920s: The Boom That Busted

1. "Ain't We Got Fun?" *Put Another Nickel in . . .*, n.d., <http://www.rienzihills.com/SING/A/aint wegotfun.htm> (August 2, 2005).

2. The Editors of Time-Life Books, *This Fabulous Century: 1920–1930* (New York: Time-Life Books, 1969), p. 280.

3. Fon W. Boardman, Jr., *The Thirties: America and the Great Depression* (New York: Henry Z. Walck, Inc., 1967), p. 2.

4. Samuel Eliot Morison, *The Oxford History of the American People* (New York: Oxford University Press, 1965), p. 940.

5. Boardman, p. 2.

6. Ibid., p. 19.

7. Korn, p. 128.

8. *The Annals of America, Volume 15: 1929–1939 The Great Depression* (Chicago and London: Encyclopaedia Britannica, Inc., 1976), p. 39.

Chapter Three Hard Times

1. Studs Terkel, *Hard Times: An Oral History of the Great Depression* (New York: Pantheon Books, 1970), p. 20.

2. Fon W. Boardman, Jr., *The Thirties: America and the Great Depression* (New York: Henry Z. Walck, Inc., 1967), p. 64.

3. Ibid., p. 31.

4. David M. Kennedy, *Freedom From Fear: The American People in Depression and War, 1929–1945* (New York: Oxford University Press, 1999), p. 67.

5. Terkel, p. 93.

6. The Editors of Time-Life Books, *This Fabulous Century: 1920–1930* (New York: Time-Life Books, 1969), p. 101.

7. T. H. Watkins, *The Great Depression: America in the 1930s* (New York: Little Brown, 1993), p. 57.

8. *The Annals of America, Volume 15: 1929–1939 The Great Depression* (Chicago and London: Encyclopaedia Britannica, Inc., 1976), p. 135.

9. Kennedy, p. 92.

Chapter Four   The New Deal Begins

1. Basil Rauch, ed., *The Roosevelt Reader: Selected Speeches, Messages, Press Conferences, and Letters of Franklin D. Roosevelt* (New York: Rinehart & Co. Inc., 1957), p. 74.

2. Studs Terkel, *Hard Times: An Oral History of the Great Depression* (New York: Pantheon Books, 1970), p. 123.

3. David M. Kennedy, *Freedom From Fear: The American People in Depression and War* (New York: Oxford University Press, 1999), p. 104.

4. Eleanor Roosevelt, *This I Remember* (New York: Harper & Brothers, 1949), p. 73.

5. Kennedy, p. 136.

6. T. H. Watkins, *The Great Depression: America in the 1930s* (New York: Little Brown, 1993), p. 143.

7. Kennedy, p. 273.

Chapter Five   The New Deal at Work

1. Studs Terkel, *Hard Times: An Oral History of the Great Depression* (New York: Pantheon Books, 1970), p. 115.

2. "The Dams and Their Builders," *The New Deal Network*, n.d., <http://newdeal.fri.org/tva/tva09.htm> (August 2, 2005).

3. T. H. Watkins, *The Great Depression: America in the 1930s* (New York: Little Brown, 1993), p. 155.

4. David M. Kennedy, *Freedom From Fear: The American People in Depression and War* (New York: Oxford University Press, 1999), p. 175.

5. Terkel, p. 425.

6. Kennedy, p. 254.

7. *The WPA Guide to Illinois: The Federal Writers' Project Guide to 1930s Illinois* (New York: Pantheon Books, 1939 [reprinted in 1983]), p. 333.

8. Kennedy, p. 254.

9. T. H. Watkins, *The Great Depression: America in the 1930s* (New York: Little Brown, 1993), p. 250.

10. Ibid., p. 249.

11. Ibid.

12. Kennedy, p. 255.

13. Watkins, p. 255.

14. Ibid.

15. Terkel, p. 58.

16. Kennedy, p. 144.

17. Watkins, p. 219.

18. Loretta Britten and Sarah Brash, eds., *Hard Times: The 30s* (Richmond, Va.: Time-Life Books, 1998), p. 29.

Chapter Six   **The New Deal and the Lingering Depression**

1. Studs Terkel, *Hard Times: An Oral History of the Great Depression* (New York: Pantheon Books, 1970), p. 274.

2. Robert Van Giezen and Albert E. Schwenk, "Compensation From Before World War I Through the Great Depression," U.S. Department of Labor: Bureau of Labor Statistics, January 30, 2003, <www.bls.gov/opub/cwc/cm20030124ar03 p10.htm> (10 October 2005).

3. David M. Kennedy, *Freedom From Fear: The American People in Depression and War* (New York: Oxford University Press, 1999), p. 312.

4. Harold Evans, *The American Century* (New York: Alfred A. Knopf, 1998), p. 278.

5. Frederick Lewis Allen, *Since Yesterday: The 1930s in America* (New York: Harper and Row, 1940), p. 157.

6. John Steinbeck, *The Grapes of Wrath* (New York: Viking Fiftieth Anniversary Issue, 1989), pp. 386–387.

7. Basil Rauch, ed., *The Roosevelt Reader: Selected Speeches, Messages, Press Conferences, and Letters of Franklin D. Roosevelt* (New York: Rinehart & Co. Inc., 1957), p. 158.

8. *The Annals of America, Volume 15: 1929–1939*

The Great Depression (Chicago and London: Encyclopaedia Britannica, Inc., 1976), p. 395.

9. David Newton Lott, ed., *The Presidents Speak: The Inaugural Addresses of American Presidents from Washington to Clinton* (New York: Henry Holt and Company, 1994), p. 285.

10. Rauch, p. 176.

11. William E. Leuchtenburg, *Franklin Roosevelt and the New Deal* (New York: Harper and Row, 1963), p. 236.

12. T. H. Watkins, *The Great Depression: America in the 1930s* (New York: Little Brown, 1993), p. 309.

13. Loretta Britten and Sarah Brash, eds., *Hard Times: The 30s* (Richmond, Va.: Time-Life Books, 1998), p. 26.

Chapter Seven   The New Dealers

1. Eleanor Roosevelt, *This I Remember* (New York: Harper & Brothers, 1949), p. 133.

2. Basil Rauch, ed., *The Roosevelt Reader: Selected Speeches, Messages, Press Conferences, and Letters of Franklin D. Roosevelt* (New York: Rinehart & Co. Inc., 1957), p. 151.

3. William Leuchtenburg, *New Deal and War* (Alexandria, Va.: Time-Life Books, 1964), p. 56.

4. Roosevelt, p. 13.

5. Leuchtenburg, p. 82.

Chapter Eight   **The Twilight and End of
the New Deal**

1. T. H. Watkins, *The Great Depression: America in the 1930s* (New York: Little Brown, 1993), p. 329.

2. Studs Terkel, *Hard Times: An Oral History of the Great Depression* (New York: Pantheon Books, 1970), p. 34.

3. David M. Kennedy, *Freedom From Fear: The American People in Depression and War* (New York: Oxford University Press, 1999), p. 176.

4. Eleanor Roosevelt, *This I Remember* (New York: Harper & Brothers, 1949), p. 136.

ballyhoo—Wild celebrating, partying.

Communism—A political system where the government owns farms, factories, and means of production.

controversy—A harsh and often public dispute.

crystal sets—Early radios used by hobbyists who had to use earphones to detect radio signals.

diagnosis—Identifying a disease or condition after examining a patient.

doling—Giving out public money in the form of welfare payments.

epic—Large in scale, grand; a movie with a cast of thousands is said to be an epic.

fluctuate—To change, as in the changing price of stocks.

frolic—To behave in a happy, carefree manner.

legacy—A tradition handed down from generation to generation.

longshoremen—Laborers who load and unload ships at docks.

plummeted—Dropped sharply.

privations—Acts of extreme suffering.

precedent—An earlier event that can be used as a standard.

rigging—Illegally fixing the results of an election.

ruinous—Events or actions which cause ruin.

scourge—A means of causing pain or punishment.

spasms—Short bursts of any kind of reaction or activity.

symbol—An object that represents something else.

unique—Individual, standing alone, or one-of-a-kind.

zany—Wildly funny, a comic character.

zeal—Great delight or enthusiasm.

Blumenthal, Karen. *Six Days in October: The Stock Market Crash of 1929*. New York: Athenium Books for Young Readers, 2002.

Cohen, Robert, ed. *Dear Mrs. Roosevelt: Letters from Children of the Great Depression*. Chapel Hill, N.C.: University of North Carolina Press, 2002.

Collier, Christopher, and James Lincoln Collier. *Progressivism, Great Depression and the New Deal: 1901–1941*. Tarrytown, N.Y.: Marshall Cavendish, 2001.

Cooper, Michael. *Dust to Eat: Drought and Depression in the 1930s*. New York: Clarion Books, 2004.

Damon, Duane. *Headin' for Better Times: The Arts of the Great Depression*. Minneapolis, Minn.: Lerner Publications, 2002.

Harris, Nathaniel. *Great Depression*. Chicago: Heinman Library, 2003.

Hesse, Karen. *Out of the Dust*. New York: Scholastic, 2000.

The American Experience: Surviving the Dust Bowl
<http://www.pbs.org/wgbh/amex/dustbowl/
peopleevents/pandeAMEX05.html>

The Library of Congress: The Great Depression and the New Deal
<http://memory.loc.gov/ammem/
wpaintro/intro01.html>

The New Deal Network
<http://newdeal.feri.org>